67 Lateral Thinking Puzzles And The King Of Riddles

The 2 Books Compilation Set Of Games And Riddles To Build Brain Cells

Karen J. Bun

This book consists of:

1. 67 Lateral Thinking Puzzles   Games And Riddles To Kill Time And Build Brain Cells

2. The King Of Riddles   The Massive Conundrum Book For Teens And Adults

67 Lateral Thinking Puzzles

Games And Riddles To Kill Time And Build Brain Cells

Karen J. Bun

Table of Contents

Introduction

Firstly, thank you for purchasing "67 Lateral Thinking Puzzles!" I sincerely hope you enjoy the following lateral puzzles provided in this book. Lateral puzzles are an excellent way to expand and grow your mind creatively. These puzzles are not simply to be solved by logical, step-by-step thinking. Instead, they are designed to mind-boggle you with a wide array of different possibilities! Originally termed by Dr. Edward De Bono in 1967, lateral thinking is a unique approach to problem-solving. This is done by using concepts that are not entirely obvious to figure out the answer. Edward described lateral thinking as the description of a process. The said process entails a creative, talented approach that considers factors that are not necessarily facts or even logical in some cases. You may even say lateral thinking is a reliance on your gut feeling, or following a mystical inclination that guides you towards what may be the right answer, or in some cases, what may be an alternative to an already existing answer. In the following puzzles you will be given a scenario with very little, but just enough information to speculate on what the answer may be. Even a "wrong" answer can be an interesting, thought-provoking one! For your peace of mind, however, the answers to said puzzles will be provided in the back of this book for you to look at once you've finished speculating. They will all be numbered accordingly from 1 to 67 so that you can match the puzzle to the puzzle answer. Now, feel free to keep reading and enjoy!

Puzzles

1. John's Trucking Disaster

John's Trucking company delivers to all the local businesses and has been doing so reliably for years. John's truck drivers travel the same route on the same roads every day without running into any issues, and they are all reliable drivers. Despite this, John's business is in need of money, and he needs to ask some of those drivers to work overtime during the holidays. As a way to make more profit this year, John decided that on Christmas Day, his drivers would continue to deliver goods. So, on Christmas Day, John sends off a few of his workers to deliver to those of the businesses that were still open on holiday. Near the end of the day, John receives a phone call informing him one of his delivery trucks has struck a bridge, and the truck has been severely damaged. Why and how did this happen on this particular day despite the fact the drivers were traveling the same route they always do previously without issue?

2. Mystery Weight Loss

A woman willingly enters an enclosed room by herself. She reaches and presses a button, and she can instantly lose twenty pounds. How was she able to do this by the simple press of a button? And where is she?

3. The Man In The Dark Room

A man sits in a dark room, enjoying himself and feeling rather entertained. In a matter of moments, he suddenly stops breathing and cannot speak. Soon after, he can speak again, and his breathing returns to normal without the Heimlich maneuver being done to help him. What happened to him and where is he?

4.   The Burglar

A wanted man committed several crimes for several months. He stole from several businesses during those months and took a decent amount of money from all of them. On one of these occasions, he was caught on the surveillance tape, and the recording was shown to the police investigating. On this tape, it clearly showed the man's face, and posters were posted all around town asking for information on the wanted man. The footage was even shown on the local TV news, asking for anyone with information on the man to catch him. However, when the man walked by the two officers aware of these burglaries, they did not react whatsoever. They barely even look his way. Why was that?

5.   The Car Accident

Just alongside a large hill, more than 45 cars were caught up in a traffic accident. The pile-up was very catastrophic. Some cars were turned over, while others had flown on top of other cars. The accident was so large that a firetruck, a police vehicle and military vehicles were involved in the crash. How could this accident come to be?

6.   Stranger In The Car

Due to a disturbance, a man helps his wife into their car, and they race desperately down the road at the top speed possible. They eventually have to stop, and the man leaves the vehicle and runs. When he returns just a few short minutes later, his wife is barely conscious and is with a stranger who is beside her in the seat. What happened to his wife while he was gone?

7.   Poisoned Iced Tea

Two best friends go out to dinner together. Both decide to order iced tea with their meal. While one drinks very slowly and talks to her friend for a few minutes between sips, the other finishes her drink very quickly and ends up drinking five iced teas while the other girl is still on her first glass. Afterward, they find out that they were poisoned, but the girl who drank the most iced tea suffers no illness while the other is taken to the hospital. Why would the girl who drank the most iced tea experience no symptoms of being poisoned while the other required immediate medical attention?

8.   Poisoned Glass

As a challenge, you are given a total of 1000 glasses. Out of all of those glasses, one contains poison, which therefore causes the juice to taste bitter. You are tasked with finding the one glass out of 1000 that contains the poison. You are provided with an antidote once you do find it, so sipping the poison to identify it is no issue. What method can be used to take the least amount of sips possible in order to find the poisoned glass without having to sip each and every one until you find it?

9.   The Forgotten Book

A lady came up to a man behind a counter and gave him a book. The man thanked her, and then said, "That will be four dollars." The lady nods and gives him the money. She then proceeds to leave without the book in hand. The man watches her leave but made no move to call her back. Why is this?

10. The Twins
One day, Carol celebrated her birthday. Two days later, her older twin, Cheryl, celebrated her birthday as well. What scenario would allow for this to be possible?

11. The Cowboy
A cowboy rode into town on a Monday. He went and rented a room to stay for three entire days and nights. When he finished his stay, he left on Monday. How did he manage to do that?

12. The Sentencing
A young, foolish teenager is put on trial and is found guilty of a minor charge. The Judge, deciding to have some fun with the man, tells him, "You can say one sentence to defend yourself in your sentencing. If you lie, you will be locked away. If you tell us the truth, you will be set free and only given a warning." What should the young man say to gain his freedom?

13. Wrong Hotel Room
A woman was settled in her hotel room when she heard a knock at her door. Confused, as she wasn't expecting anyone, she gets up and answers the door. On the other side, there was a man who seemed surprised to see her answer. "My apologies, madam! I thought this was my room! Sorry to disturb you." He left immediately after and the woman returned into her room to call hotel security. Why would she suspect anything?

14.   The Triangle

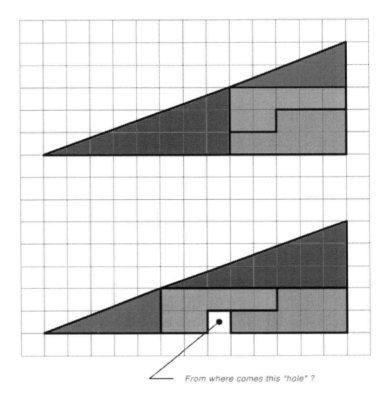

From where comes this "hole" ?

Here are two triangles made up of equal parts. However, the bottom one is missing a box. How is this possible?

15. True Love At A Funeral

A young lady attended her mother's funeral. While she was there, she met a mysterious love interest. She was utterly charmed by him, as he was the man of her dreams and she has been on her own for a long time. She falls madly in love with him instantly just after one day of the meeting. A few days after the funeral the girl murders her own sister. What reason would she have of doing this?

16. The Murderer

The police department receives a phone call providing an anonymous tip about a suspected murderer, stating that the murderer is hiding out in a house playing a game of poker. The police immediately raid the house mentioned in the tip. They do not, however, know anything about the appearance of the suspected murderer. All they know is that he is a man, and his name is Michael. Upon entering the house, they see a taxi driver, a blacksmith, a plumber, and a fireman all playing poker. Without hesitating, the police officers arrest the fireman without a word or interaction with the others. How would they know that the fireman was the murderer without knowing anything about the murderer's appearance?

17. Thirsty

A man lies in his own bed and passes away in the comfort of his own home due to thirst. Why would he allow this to happen?

18. Clean Faces

Two best friends, Tom and Henry, are playing on the school playground during recess. When recess is over, and the bell rings, the two boys run back to class. On their way a giant gust of wind causes a mass of dirt to be thrown in both of their faces. Tom's face is absolutely filthy, while Henry's is still miraculously clean. However, it is Henry that rushes to the bathroom to clean his face, while Tom returns to class without doing so. Assuming that both boys care equally about their own hygiene, why would they each react this way?

19. Fingerprints

Almost every single night, a man enters the police station after hours and destroys hundreds upon hundreds of fingerprints. Even so, that man has never been charged or caught of a crime. How is this possible?

20. Pool Balls

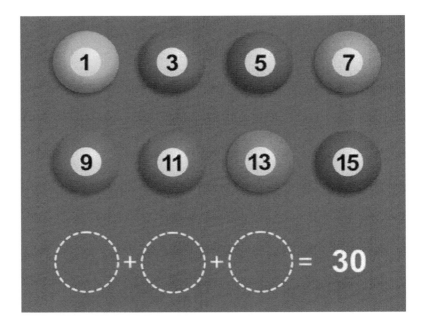

You have been given the following pool balls. Using the numbers shown in the following picture (1, 3, 5, 7, 9, 11, 13, and 15), you need to select three in order to add to 30. What balls can you use?

21. The Philosopher

A careless philosopher forgot to wind up his clock. He now has no way of attaining the time as he doesn't prefer to keep up with technology and prefers to live with little influence from the outside world. He has no radio, no TV, no telephone, no internet, or any other means of getting the time besides walking to his friend's house to get it from him. He sets out to do this and walks to his friend's house. It is a straight desert road, and the travel is only a few miles. He stays there for the night and walks home the following morning. He is then able to set his clock to the correct time. The philosopher did not bring anything to this friend's house in order to keep track of time in any way, nor did he have his friend time him. How was he able to estimate the time that passed on his walk home from his friend's in order to set the clock?

22. Found Guilty

A man is brought to court after being accused of murdering his wife after his wife was reported missing and has now been missing for a month. The man claims that his wife has left him, leaving nothing behind so that he would not be able to find her and that he is not guilty of murder. As part of his defense, his lawyer asks everyone present to look to the back. "To prove that my client is not guilty, I have asked his wife to enter the doors in just a minute to prove that she has, in fact, not killed!" The entire jury, the judge, and everyone hearing the case looks to the door, only to see no one enter. After a moment, the lawyer claims, "See! This only proves that you are uncertain that my client could have killed his wife. Otherwise, you would not have bothered looking!" Almost immediately after, the jury all decides that the accused man is guilty. Why is that?

23. Millionaire

A nice gentleman named Mr. Johnson buys up $5 worth of packages full of food and supplies from the United States, only to sell them for a mere $1 in Africa to those in need. He continues doing this for a very long time in order to help out the country. He eventually goes on to become a Millionaire with this plan. How does he manage this?

24. A Load of Wood

Driving down the road, a man miraculously came across a man driving a large truck with a load of wood in the back. His truckload contained wood that was neither straight nor crooked. How is this possible?

25. The Short Line

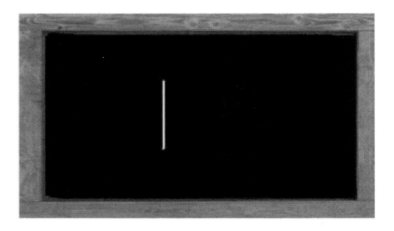

You are provided with this chalkboard with the line already drawn on in chalk. You are tasked with making this line shorter, but you may not erase any part of the line. How will you do it?

26. Rectangular House

A man decided to build a house, giving each and every side of the house a fantastic view facing south for his family to look out. After finishing this house, he goes outside and comes face to face with a bear. What kind of bear is it?

27. The Window Cleaner

A window cleaner is working on the 34th floor of a massive skyscraper. While cleaning the windows, he accidentally falls. In this instance, he is wearing absolutely no safety equipment. He does not have a harness and has nothing to slow or soften his fall. However, despite this, he sustains no injuries whatsoever. How did he manage not to get injured from this terrible fall?

28. Three Rooms

You come to three rooms and have to choose to open one of their doors and go inside. The first is filled with flames, the second is filled with tigers who have not eaten in three years, and the third and last room is filled with three hitmen all tasked with terminating you. Which room is the wisest to choose?

29. Three Days

You must find a way to say three consecutive days without saying Monday, Wednesday, or Friday in any of the combinations. How could you do this while still using only English words?

30. The Goldfish

A young girl has a pet goldfish that she adores very much. One day she looks in the bowl and finds that the fish is swimming very weakly and has lost all its energy. Devastated, she takes the goldfish to the vet to help her beloved pet regain its strength. The vet takes a look at her goldfish and quickly returns with the goldfish swimming much better. The girl was thrilled, but this seems suspicious. How did the vet manage to get the goldfish swimming well again?

31. Billy

Little, four-year-old Billy, had both of his parents pass away recently. His new caretaker decided to put Billy on a train on his own to get to his new home in the country. Unfortunately, Billy could not speak or write and could not tell anyone on the train his destination so that they can make sure he gets there on his own. Since this is the case, his guardian writes his destination on a little note and tie it on a string around his neck. Despite this note, Billy never manages to get to his destination. Why is this?

32. Forecast

A man sits at home and watches the weather forecast on his TV. It is just after midnight that the man hears they are expecting rain for the next two days straight, but after 72 hours it will be bright, sunny and warm again. The man laughs and says, "They're wrong again!" How could he predict that for sure? Is he psychic?

33. East and West

While in the North Pole, it is absolutely impossible to look North. The same goes for the South Pole, where it is impossible to look South. With this being the case, where in the world would you have to be in order to be able to look North or South, but not be able to look East or West?

34. Fallen Man

A detective is called to a possible murder scene. Once he arrives, he sees that a man has fallen from an abandoned building, presumably from one of the many windows. His colleagues argue that the man likely did this to himself and this is not a case of murder. The detective pondered on this and traveled inside the building to investigate. He stood on the first floor in front of the window that faces the man and lits a cigarette. After a while, he puts out his cigarette, opens the window and throws it out before closing it again. He does this on the second floor as well as the third floor. After this, he returns back to his colleagues certain that the man was indeed murdered. How did he find this out during his smoke break?

35. The Strings

You hold two different strings of different lengths. You also have a book of matches. If you lit one end of the longer string it will burn for about 10 minutes. If the shorter string is burned it will take only about 1 minute. Using these strings you have to attempt to measure precisely 5 and a half minutes of time. There are a few tools you are unable to use as well. You do not have scissors or anything to cut the string. You also do not have the ability to bend the string correctly in half as it is too rigid. You also cannot accurately estimate the half point of either of the strings just by looking at them because it would still not be entirely accurate. How can you measure the five minutes and thirty seconds?

36. The Wine Bottle

You have both a used wine bottle and the cork left over. If you were to put a small coin within the bottle and insert the cork back into the neck of the bottle, how would you be able to retrieve that coin without breaking the bottle or removing the cork again?

37. The Coffee and the Fly

A woman walks into a cafe and sits down at one of the booths. Soon enough, a waitress comes by and takes her order. She asks for only a cup of coffee. Shortly after the waitress returns with the coffee and heads back to the kitchen. A few minutes later, the woman notices that a fly has found its way into her coffee cup. Politely, the woman motions the waitress to come back and asks for another fresh cup of coffee. The waitress takes her cup and returns to the kitchen. A few minutes later she returns, saying, "There you go. I poured you a new cup of coffee. No fly this time." She leaves the cup on the table and turns to head back to the kitchen. She only makes a few steps before her customer calls her back. "Hey! This is the same cup! You only removed the fly and gave me the same one!" While assuming that the coffee is still hot and the coffee machine is not in view of the customer, how would she be able to tell it was the same coffee?

38. Blindfolded Scott

A blindfolded boy named Scott sits in front of a rotating tray. The tray contains four identical individual glasses. Some are upside down, and others are right side up. However, he is not aware of which is which in this situation. The glasses are placed in rows of two, forming a square. A bartender named Mary challenges Scott to rearrange all the glasses so that they all match and are all either right side up or upside down. However, he does have some rules to follow. Any two glasses may be touched in order to see which way they are placed. Mary shall help him locate and touch the glasses. Scott can go ahead and flip either both glasses, one of them, or flip neither. Mary will then spin the tray to a random number of degrees to provide new and random positions of the glasses. This will continue until Scott manages to get all four glasses in the same orientation, at which point Mary will let him know. In this scenario, Scott does not want to exceed five turns of the tray before getting the right answer. What strategy can he use to do this?

39. Manholes

Manhole covers are all made in a circular shape as opposed to a square because they have a commanding advantage. What are the circular-shaped covers preferred for?

40. The Long Fishing Rod

A man purchases a brand new fishing rod and needs to take the bus home. He stands in line and attempts to board the bus. Unfortunately, they measure the rod, and he is informed that it is too long to bring on the bus. The maximum length of an item is 4 feet, and his fishing rod is 5 feet. The man sadly returns to the store to return the item. Thankfully, the cashier proposes a smart way to be still able to board with the fishing rod. The man is skeptical as he does not want to break or bend the fishing rod to do this. However, the cashier is able to suggest a way that avoids doing this. What is his proposal?

41. The Chemist

A chemist is murdered in his lab. The crime scene leaves no solid clues for his murder except for one. The chemist left a piece of paper behind. On that paper, was a list of several different substances. These substances were nickel, carbon, oxygen, lanthanum, and sulfur. After collecting this piece of evidence, the police looked for their next clue. They checked with everyone that came by that lab that entire day. His nephew Nicolas came by, his lab partner Gina came by, his wife came by, and his friend James came by. They did not even have to call them in for questioning. The officers knew immediately who the murderer was. It was Nicolas. How did they come to this conclusion so quickly?

42. Man in the Field

A man mysteriously lies face down in a field, deceased, and wearing a backpack. A few moments before his death, he became aware of his approaching demise. However, there were no objects of importance in the field nor on him or in his backpack. He was not killed by a person or an animal, and he was perfectly healthy and not ailed in any way. He did not die of old age, stroke, or of any health condition or allergy. He was also not killed by a lightning strike or any other act of God. So, how did he end up dying and how did he know it would happen?

43. The Wish

A manservant works for his master tirelessly for thirty years. He is loyal and a good man to his master. After those thirty years, his master falls ill and is certain that he will not recover. With his faithful manservant at his side, he admits that he has extraordinary powers and would like to grant his servant one wish before he passes away as a thank you for his service. The manservant is very thankful, but cannot decide on the spot so his master gives him one day to decide on what he would like to wish. He goes home and speaks to his wife about it, who then is overjoyed at the possibility. "Wish for a son! We have been childless for too many years! Now is our chance!" The manservant considers this. Then, he goes and speaks with his mother, who is blind. She is also overjoyed and says, "Please, son! Ask for my sight back so that I may see the world again!" The manservant also considers this. Then, he speaks with his father, who has been awfully poor his whole life and is now too old to make any sort of living. "Please, son! Ask for the riches our family has always had to live without!" The manservant considers this as well and is torn. What will he end up choosing? Is there an option that allows him to make everyone happy?

44. Mountain Trip Accident

Mr. and Mrs. Gold took a vacation to the mountains for their anniversary. They hiked together to the top of the mountain. Unfortunately, only Mr. Gold would end up returning. Upon his return he reports the death of his wife, stating that his wife accidentally fell to her death from the edge of a cliff during their hike and he was unable to save her in time. The police officers end up arresting Mr. Gold shortly after searching his hotel room for the murder of his wife, has found substantial evidence that he intended to murder his wife. What could they have seen that suggested this?

45. St. Ives

On his way to St. Ives, a man happens upon a plentiful family. He came across a man with 6 wives, each carrying 6 sacks filled with 6 mother cats, all with 6 kittens each. That makes one man with plenty of wives and sacks filled with cats and kittens in tow. How many of them are going to St. Ives?

46. The Equal Squares

You are given a square and told to divide it into four different equal parts. There are two simple enough ways to do this as you can see below. However, there are 8 other different ways to do this. What are those other ways?

47. Truck Driver

A police officer is driving on the highway and notices a truck driver clearly traveling in the wrong direction. Instead of pulling over and setting him straight, he ignores him and keeps going. Why would he ignore this?

48. Plane Crash

A terrible plane crash occurred in the mountains. Forty people were on board, none surviving. They were found later the same day, but no survivors were buried. Why is that?

49. Snowball

A man sat alone in the comfort of his home in front of his fireplace. It was a very cold, winter evening, and snow covered his entire backyard. As he sat and relaxed, he was suddenly disturbed by a snowball that came crashing through his window. Understandably angry that he was now exposed to the cold, he ran up to the window and saw three of the neighborhood boys in his backyard. They were all laughing and running away as they joked around with each other. The man was able to identify the boys as three brothers by the names Jack Smith, Mark Smith, and Tom Smith. As they were already running away and he didn't feel like chasing them, the man closed up the broken window and went to bed. The very next morning, he went out to retrieve his newspaper and found a paper note stuck to his door. It said, "? Smith. He threw the snowball and broke your window." The man instantly knew from this note which brother it was that broke his window. How did he know?

50. The Sand Smuggler

A strange man crosses the Mexican border regularly every single day while only riding a bicycle. Every time he does, he carries two bags full of sand with him. The customs officers check the bag, only to find only sand every single time. They suspect that he is smuggling something but to their frustration, they can never find any proof, so he always gets away with it. What is he hiding?

51. Guilty Husband

A man has just murdered his wife. When he returned home, he received a call from the police stating that his wife has been murdered and her body was only found at the scene of the crime. The man fakes his shock, and the police ask him to come to the scene of the crime right away. The man jumps in his car and gets there as soon as possible, only to be arrested the moment he arrives for the murder of his wife. How did the police know it was him?

52. Who Stole The Money?

A man left a $500 bill on his dresser before leaving for his daily routine. When he came home that night, he was irritated to find that the $500 was now gone. He had three employees that could be responsible: the cook, the maid, and the electrician. He went to question the cook first, who claimed that he indeed did see the $500 bill and put it under a book for safekeeping. The man returned to his dresser and saw the book there. Looking under it, he saw that it was no longer there! He then went to question the maid. She immediately claimed that she moved the bill inside the book between the first and second page while she was cleaning his dresser and saw it there. The man went back and checked the book, and saw nothing there. He then spoke with the electrician, who later claimed he saw it poking out of the book and moved it to page 2 and 3 for safekeeping. Enraged, the man immediately fires the electrician and demands his money back. How did he know it was him?

53. Two Cars

Two cars are traveling down the center of town. One of them is a man driving a little red car. The man driving the red car overtakes the black car as it is traveling too slow for his liking. The driver, while doing this, misjudged the amount of time he had to pass before he would get in the way of oncoming traffic. The black car swerves into a local shop to avoid an accident and crashes through the window. The red car swerves as well out of the way of the oncoming traffic and successfully avoids all the oncoming cars without harming himself. In the black car, however, there is one dead man found after the accident. Despite this, the driver of the green car is not charged with manslaughter. Why not?

54. Cell Window

Carl is locked in a jail cell. The ground is made of dirt, and he has a shovel. He also has a cell window, but it is just out of reach at his height. Carl is trying to plan an escape that takes less than two days because he will not have access to food or water during his journey. He considered digging a tunnel in the dirt, but it will still take more than two days, and he will not make it. How else will he be able to escape?

55. Captain's Missing Ring

A Japanese ship is leaving port. The Captain grabs some oil to grease up some parts of the ship. Before he leaves, he takes off his ring and leaves it behind so that he won't lose it or damage it. He leaves it on his dresser in his cabin. He returns ten minutes later only to find that his ring is gone. He asks his crew about the missing ring. His cook says "I was busy in the kitchen, making tonight's dinner for everyone in the crew." He speaks to the engineer. He says, "I was working hard in the engine room to make sure everything was running smoothly before we leave port." He talks to the seaman then. He says, "I was on the mast correcting the flag. Someone had accidentally attached it upside down and had to be corrected." The Captain immediately knows who is lying about their whereabouts. Who is lying? How did he know?

56. First Day of School

On the first day back to school, the science teacher was murdered. All four suspects turned out to be all fellow employees at the school as no one else had entered the building that early in the morning. The first suspect was the principal. He claims that he was in his office at the time of the crime, preparing for the new school year. The second suspect was the history teacher. She says that she was preparing for her midterm tests to give to her students. The third suspect was the landscaper. He says that he was mowing the lawn before the students arrive. The fourth and final suspect was the Track and Field coach. She says that she was setting up to do some drills outside with her students. The police know immediately after questioning everyone who is guilty. It is the history teacher. How did they figure this out?

57. The Princess's Hand In Marriage

A poor man with no land or anything to his name falls in love with the princess of the Kingdom he lives in. Desperate for her love, he courts her in secret, and they fall in love with each other. They come to the King, her father, together and present her wish to marry him. The King is not at all pleased with this proposal but does not want to appear unfair and then proposes an alternative. He will allow the poor man to marry his daughter if he wins a game of chance. He will put two pieces of paper in a bowl. One will say, "Exile." If he picks this one, he will be banished from the Kingdom and never see the Princess ever again. The other piece of paper will say, "Marriage." If he picks this one, the marriage will continue. The poor man happily agrees as he believes any chance is better than no chance at all. However, later that night, the hopeful man overhears the King talking to one of his men. He says, "I will be writing 'Exile' on both of those papers. There's no way that man deserves my daughter's hand in marriage!" The man is unaffected and doesn't lose his confidence as he is sure he knows how to turn this in his favor. What does he do to earn the Princess's hand in marriage regardless of the King working against him?

58. Teaspoons of Sugar

You are given three cups, sugar, and a teaspoon. You are tasked with distributing 10 teaspoons of sugar in three different cups. The rule is that there has to be an odd amount of teaspoons in each of the cups. How can you do this while still adding up to 10, an even number?

59. Haircut

A man arrives in a small town and is in desperate need of a haircut. Since he is in such a small town, they only have two barbers across the street from each other. He has to decide between the two by guessing who would give a better cut. The first barber has a unique shop that is clean and tidy. His hair is also done very nicely as well. The second barber has a chaotic, messy shop and a terrible haircut. The first shop also charges a reasonable price, while the second shop has the audacity to be slightly more expensive. What shop should he choose and why?

60. Bearded Boy

In a small town, there lived a boy and his parents. The teenaged boy, one night, asks for his parent's permission to go visit a friend nearby. They agreed that he could as long as he would be back by the time the sun rises. The boy agreed and went on his way. When he left, he had a clean-shaven face. When he returned, however, he has managed to grow a beard since the previous time he saw his parents fully. How did he manage this?

61. Anniversary Discount

As a promotional deal, a local restaurant offers a half discount to couples who dine on their anniversary. Their prices are high-end, and they want to bring in some new customers. In order to prevent any scammers from claiming the promotion when it isn't truly their anniversary, the restaurant requires proof of their wedding date. One couple happens to come in on a Thursday and forgot to bring proof. Instead of paying full price, they request to speak to the manager. The manager comes to talk with the couple and asks them to describe their wedding day. The wife answers, "Oh, it was a wonderful Sunday afternoon. The sun was shining; the birds were chirping! It was the happiest day of our lives!" The man agrees, "Yes, and it's now our 28th anniversary." The store manager denies their request as he knows now that it could not be their anniversary. How did he know this?

62. The Sheep

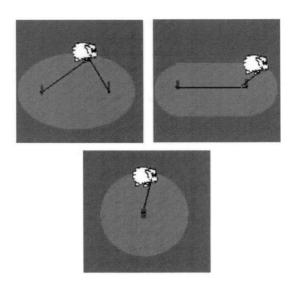

As shown below, when tying a sheep on one peg, it will eat a circle of grass. If he is tied to two different pegs, he will eat an oval. The sheep will eat in the shape of a longer oval if the rope is tightened between two pegs, connected by a ring to the rope tied to the sheep as shown below. In order to get the sheep to eat in the shape of a square, what would you need to do?

63. Wise Man

A wise man lives in a small village in his entire life. The wise man is trusted by many to give advice on their difficult problems and to settle disagreements peacefully and fairly. To test the wise man, some tourist men set out to test his abilities. Behind their back, they hold a dove so that the wise man cannot see. They then ask the wise man, "Is the dove I hold alive, or dead?" The wise man shakes his head and concludes, "I cannot answer your question correctly." Why does he say this?

64. Heaven

A man passes away and goes to heaven after the conclusion of his life. When he arrived, he was amazed to see everyone that he happened to recognize and shockingly none were wearing clothes! To his amazement, he was able to identify Adam and Eve immediately in the crowd without having any idea what they look like. How did he figure out who they were without any knowledge of their physical attributes?

65. The Concrete Room

A man stands in a room. The room has no doors or windows. The walls are also made of 6-inch thick concrete. The floor is even made of concrete. Despite this, the man is easily able to leave with ease. How does he do this?

66. Surgeon

A man and his son are driving on the highway, and they are suddenly struck by another vehicle. They swerve into the ditch, and the son is severely injured. After being rushed to the hospital, the surgeon is shocked to see the boy and exclaims, "I can't operate on this boy! He is my son!" How could this be?

67. Painted Cubes

Below, there are three different shapes containing squares. Most of the space is painted, but they all have parts that are left white. Which of the shapes are painted the most?

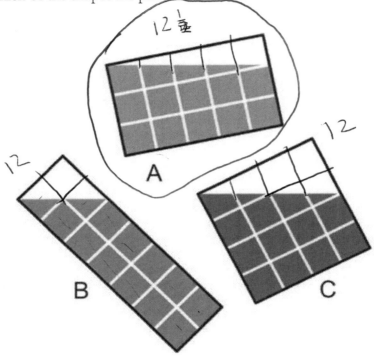

Puzzle Answers

1.   John's Trucking Disaster

Answer: Since it was Christmas Day, John's delivery trucks were not able to deliver to very many businesses as most had closed down for the day. After the driver was able to make all his stops, his truck was empty as he was not given very many supplies to transport. Since his truck was empty, his truck had a higher profile than it usually does. Due to this, the truck was able to hit a bridge it never has before on the way back.

2. Mystery Weight Loss

Answer: The enclosed room the woman enters is actually an elevator. When she presses the button, and the elevator goes into motion downward, the acceleration causes her to temporarily lower her apparent weight, effectively helping her briefly lose twenty pounds!

3. The Man In The Dark Room

Answer: The man is actually watching a movie at the movie theatre. He sips his favorite soda and subsequently chokes on a small chunk of ice. Briefly, this causes him to be unable to breathe. However, it doesn't take long before the ice melts, and he is able to return to his normal breathing.

4. The Burglar

Answer: The man walked by the two officers having already been arrested and in jail. The two officers were at the prison to get a statement from the man regarding his upcoming trial.

5. The Car Accident

Answer: All the vehicles were influenced by a child playing with his toys in his sandbox.

6. The Stranger In The Car

Answer: The man and his wife were expecting a baby. They drove to the hospital over the speed limit as she was already in labor. When they arrived, he ran to get a wheelchair to bring her into the hospital. When he returned, she had given birth to their child already.

7. Poisoned Iced Tea

Answer: The poison wasn't in the iced tea itself. It was actually in the ice cubes. Since the girl who was successfully poisoned drank so slowly, the ice had time to melt and release into her drink. As for the other girl, she drank so quickly the ice was not able to melt fast enough to release the poison.

8. Poisoned Glass

Answer: The best method is to divide the 1000 glasses into two groups of 500. Now, you must choose one of these groups and carefully pour one drop of each glass into another glass so that the 500 drops fill another glass. Now, take a sip and see if it tastes bitter in any way. If it does or doesn't, it will indicate which group of the 500 contains the poison. Once you have identified this, you may divide that group of 500 into groups of 250 and repeat the same process. You may continue doing this until you narrow it down to just one glass. This glass will contain the poison.

9. The Forgotten Book

Answer: The lady was not purchasing a book. She was actually only returning an overdue library book and paying the late fee.

10. The Twins

Answer: When Carol and Cheryl's mother went into labor, she was traveling by boat. The older twin, Cheryl, was born very early on March 1st. The boat then crossed time zones, therefore causing Carol to be born on February 28th instead. When it happens to be a leap year, the twins celebrate their birthdays two entire days apart.

11. The Cowboy

Answer: His horse's name happened also to be "Monday."

12. The Sentencing

Answer: The man could have two different appropriate responses."It's certain that you will lock me away." You could also say, "I am lying right now."

13. Wrong Hotel Room

Answer: The woman suspected that if that man truly believed that it was his room, he would have attempted to use his key to get in, not knock! Therefore, she instantly suspects that he was attempting a robbery and was merely checking if anyone was in the room.

14. The Triangle

Answer: The image does appear like a triangle, but isn't quite a triangle. The top image has a bowed *in* hypotenuse, while the bottom image is bowed *outwards*. If you look carefully, the red and green triangles do not have the exact same ratios, resulting in different hypotenuses and a different angle, eventually resulting in that space on the bottom picture.

15. True Love At A Funeral

Answer: The woman murdered her sister in hopes that the man would return and attend the funeral so that she would be able to see him again.

16. The Murderer

Answer: The fireman happened to be the only man in the room. The rest of the poker players were, in fact, women.

17. Thirst

Answer: The man lives in a houseboat. He is currently in the middle of a saltwater ocean, unable to get fresh water.

18. Clean Faces

Answer: Tom saw Henry's clean face and assumed his face was in the same condition. The same occurred from Henry's point of view when he saw the dirty state of Tom's face.

19. Fingerprints

Answer: The man is a janitor who cleans overnight at the police station.

20. Pool Balls

Answer: The number 9 is actually supposed to be a 6 in the game of pool. By turning it around, you can use a 6, 11, and 13 to add to 30.

21. The Philosopher

Answer: Before the philosopher leaves, he winds his clock and sets it to a random time, say 9:00, for example. This is not the correct time, but it will help him estimate when he returns by tracking the amount of time his entire trip takes. As soon as he arrives, the philosopher looks at his friend's clock, which says 7:15. He stays overnight and then looks at the clock one more time before leaving. At that time it was 10:15, 15 hours later. When he returns home, his clock now says 12:40. The philosopher can now use this to subtracting the time it was when he left. He knows he has been gone for 15 hours and 40 minutes, meaning he spent 40 minutes walking and it takes him 20 minutes to walk one way. He will now know to set the time to 20 minutes after what time it was when he left his friend's house, which is 10:35.

22. Found Guilty

Answer: The accused man was the one exception of everyone that looked to the door. He was certain that she would not enter when his lawyer claimed this because he had indeed killed her.

23. Millionaire

Answer: The man started his sales as a billionaire and eventually became only a millionaire from the lost profit.

24. A Load of Wood

Answer: The wood was in the form of sawdust, therefore making it neither straight nor crooked.

25. The Short Line

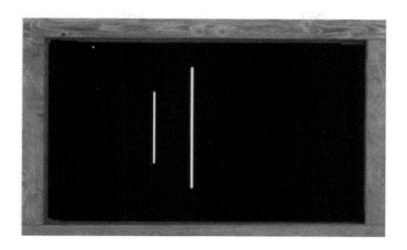

In order to make the line shorter without erasing any portion of it, you can draw another line beside it, but longer. The longer line will then make the first line the shorter of the line.

26. Rectangular House

Answer: He comes face to face with a polar bear. Only a house located in the North Pole would be able to have every side facing south.

27. Window Cleaner

Answer: The window cleaner is only cleaning the inside of the windows and therefore has no need for a safety harness.

28. Three Rooms

Answer: The second room. The Tigers have all starved to death.

29. Three Days

Answer: Yesterday, today, and tomorrow. You could also say Christmas Eve, Christmas and Boxing day or another similar combination of holidays.

30. The GoldFish

Answer: The vet was able to quickly see that the goldfish was passing away from old age. To spare the girl's feelings, he was able to switch the goldfish for a new one and return it to her.

31. Billy

Answer: Billy, as his name hints at, is, in fact, a goat. Due to this, Billy decided to eat the paper with his destination written on it. This prevents anyone from understanding where his destination is.

32. Forecast

Answer: In 72 hours, there will not even be any daylight, so it is therefore impossible to be bright and sunny.

33. East and West

Answer: If you are in the very center of the Earth's core, you would be able to look North and South, but you could not look East or West.

34. Fallen Man

Answer: While the detective was inside the building, he was able to confirm that every single window facing the man was closed. He had to open each one before throwing out his cigarette butt. Anyone that would have accidentally fallen out of the window or done this to themselves would not have closed the window behind them before their fall. The murderer must have locked it behind them.

35. The Strings

Answer: To measure exactly five minutes and thirty seconds, you will have to light both ends of the longer string first. You will allow both ends to burn consistently until they meet in the middle at five minutes. Immediately after both flames meet, you will have to do the same to the second string to measure the thirty seconds.

36. Wine Bottle

Answers: You can do this by inserting the cork into the bottle so that it is not blocking the neck. You can then shake the bottle until the coin is able to fall out.

37. The Coffee and the Fly

Answer: The woman was able to notice immediately that it was the same coffee because she had added sugar while the waitress wasn't looking. When she was given back, she sipped it and found that it was already sweet and sugar was already added.

38. Blindfolded Scott

Answer: Scott can complete the task in five rounds as follows:

Round 1: Choose any two glasses that are diagonally opposite each other. He will flip both so that they are right side up if they are not already. This will mean that at least two glasses are right side up.

Round 2: Scott will then choose two glasses that are alongside each other (adjacent). At least one will be right side up from the last round. If one of the two adjacent is upside down, turn that one right side up. There are now at least three cups right side up.

Round 3: Scott will now choose two glasses that are diagonally opposite once again. If one is turned downwards, turn it up, and all four glasses will be right side up. If both are right side up, turn one upside down, and there will be two upside-down adjacents to each other.

Round 4: Choose two adjacent glasses and flip them both. If both were the same orientation, then all four glasses will now be flipped the same way. If they were not flipped the same way, there would be two glasses that are upside down diagonally across from each other.

Round 5: Scott will choose any two glasses that are diagonally opposite and reverse both of them. All four glasses will now be the same orientation.

39. Manholes

Answer: Unlike square or rectangular covers, circular covers run no risk of sliding through the hole diagonally. Circular manhole covers can also be rolled for easy transport.

40. The Long Fishing Rod

Answer: The man was able to purchase a box from the store that was 3 x 4. He was then able to place the fishing rod inside the box diagonally to meet the bus's item length requirement.

41. The Chemist

Answer: The substances listed on the piece of paper was the chemist's clue for the officers. When combining the abbreviations of those substances, it will spell out Nicolas. His nephew is, therefore, the killer.

42. Man in the Field

Answer: The man was skydiving and his parachute failed, therefore explaining how he knew of his death moments before it happened.

43. The Wish

Answer: The manservant could tell his master this: "I wish for my mother to be able to see her grandson swing from a swingset made out of gold." Other similar answers could apply as well.

44. Mountain Trip Accident

Answer: The police found in Mr. Gold's room that he had only purchased one return plane ticket, thus suggesting that he never planned to bring his wife back home with him.

45. St. Ives

Answer: Only the one man is said to be traveling to St. Ives. He just happened to come across that man and his wives and cats on the way!

46. Equal Squares

Answer: Here are the other 8 ways to divide the square equally.

47. Truck Driver

Answer: The truck driver was walking on the side of the road and was not actually driving the wrong way on the road. Therefore, the police officer had no reason to pull him over.

48. Plane Crash

Answer: There were no survivors, and even if there were, they wouldn't bury those that were still alive!

49. Snowball

Answer: The note was a tricky clue for the man to figure out! The ? hinted that he needed to "Question Mark Smith" about the thrown snowball, meaning that Mark Smith was the culprit he was looking for!

50. The Sand Smuggler

Answer: This clever fellow is in fact smuggling bicycles! He distracts the customs officers with the simple bags of sand in order to divert their attention off of the different bikes he rides every day!

51. Guilty Husband

Answer: The police never once informed the man where the scene of the crime was. Since the man was able to bring himself to the scene of the crime without any instructions or indication of where it was confirmed that he was the one that had murdered her.

52. Who Stole the Money?

Answer: The electrician couldn't have moved the bill to between pages 2 and 3. The man checked this when the maid claimed to have wedged it between 1 and 2. With page 1 and 2 facing each other, pages 2 and 3 would not be. If the electrician was telling the truth, he would have said he moved it between pages 3 and 4. Besides, why would he move it between different pages anyway when he could have just pushed it further between the pages it was already between in the first place?

53. Two Cars

Answer: The black car was a hearse and was already carrying a dead man aboard as they were on the way to his funeral. Nobody was harmed during the accident.

54. Cell Window

Carl will be able to escape by creating a pile of dirt with his shovel. He can climb this pile in order to reach the cell window. He will then be able to climb out of the window and escape.

55. Captain's Missing Ring

Answer: The Captain knew the seaman was lying because the Japanese flag cannot be hung upside down. Only one dot is in the middle of their flag so that it can be hung in any way and still be upright.

56. First Day Of School

Answer: The police knew that the history teacher killed the science teacher because she claimed that she was giving her students a midterm test. This was not a possibility because it was the first day of the school year.

57. The Princess's Hand In Marriage

Answer: The man draws one of the papers and immediately tears it up. He then asks the King if he can see the other paper to indicate which one he pulled. The King, baffled, will take out the other paper. This will, of course, read, "Exile." This will then influence everyone to believe that the paper he initially drew would have said, "Marriage." Then the King will allow the marriage to not appear like a fool in front of his subjects.

58. Teaspoons of Sugar

Answer: You will need to put seven teaspoons in one cup. Then, you will need to put one teaspoon in one, and two in another as shown below.

59. Haircut

Answer: The second shop. It is safe to assume that usually, barbers do not attempt to cut their own hair. Even though the second barber had a messy shop, it was evident that his haircut was a reflection of the first barber's skills and the first barber had an excellent cut done by the second barber. Therefore, the second barber was the right choice. His prices are more because his quality of work is much higher.

60. Bearded Boy

Answer: The small town the family lives in is the town of Barrow in Alaska, located in the north of the United States. In this particular town, the sun sets in the middle of November and does not rise again for about 65 days. The boy is away for this entire time, and by the time he returns, he has managed to grow a beard.

61. Anniversary Discount

Answer: The store manager knew one simple fact. Every 28 years, the calendar repeats. Since it was Thursday on that particular day, he knew that it was impossible for them to have been married any day except Thursday. Still, they claimed they married on a Sunday, which therefore proved that they were lying.

62. The Sheep

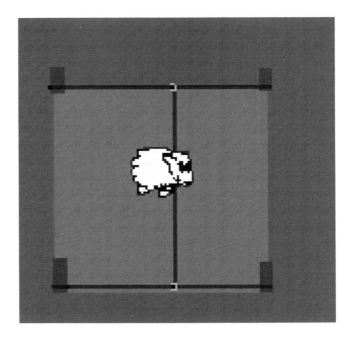

Answer: In order to do this, you can install four pegs in the shape of a square, with one peg at each corner. On two sides, tighten a rope between the pegs, forming two lines. Use the third rope and connect it to both of the existing ropes with rings so that the sheep is secured between the two sides.

63. Wise Man

Answer: The wise man was right to answer this. It would be impossible to answer the question as the men were only there to prove him wrong and he knew this from the start. The dove was alive, but he knew if he were to answer that it was alive, they would kill it to prove him incorrect. If he said that it was dead, the dove would then be set free to prove him wrong. No matter what he answered, it could be proven wrong, so instead, he chose not to respond.

64. Heaven

Answer: The man knew it was Adam and Eve because they were the only people present that did not have a naval, meaning that they were not born from a woman's womb.

65. The Concrete Room

Answer: There are several answers that work with this scenario. First, the man is in a basement and is able to walk up the stairs to another level that has a door. The second is that the room only has three walls, so he is able to walk out. It never indicates that there are four walls. The third is that he walks out through the doorway since there is no door as it also never indicates there is no doorway where a door should be. The fourth is that he leaves through the window frame, as there is no actual window.

66. Surgeon

Answer: The surgeon also happened to be the boy's mother! It was never indicated that the surgeon was also supposedly the father.

67. Painted Cubes

Answer: All the cubes have an equal amount of space painted.

Conclusion

Thank you for making it through "67 Lateral Puzzles." Hopefully, you enjoyed the book and were able to kill some time and some boredom with the previous puzzles. Hopefully, this book was also able to help expand your mind, and open it creatively in order to solve future problems. Lateral thinking is an excellent way to do this, and we hope you continue reading and trying to solve lateral puzzles in the future. The next step to further your mind is to look for even more puzzles online, or in other books. In addition to that, we also hope that you had some fun trying to solve all of the puzzles included in this book! Thank you, everyone, for reading.

Finally, if you enjoyed this book, a review on Amazon is absolutely appreciated.

Catch us on Facebook www.facebook.com/bluesourceandfriends

Don't forget to claim your FREE book
https://tinyurl.com/karenbrainteasers

Karen J. Bun

The King Of Riddles

The Massive Conundrum Book For Teens And Adults

Karen J. Bun

Contents

Bluesource And Friends

This book is brought to you by Bluesource And Friends, a happy book publishing company.
Our motto is **"Happiness Within Pages"**
We promise to deliver amazing value to readers with our books.
We also appreciate honest book reviews from our readers.
Connect with us on our Facebook page
www.facebook.com/bluesourceandfriends and stay tuned to our latest book promotions and free giveaways.

Don't forget to claim your FREE book

https://tinyurl.com/karenbrainteasers

Also check out our best seller book
https://tinyurl.com/lateralthinkingpuzzles

Introduction

Congratulations on getting *The King of Riddles* and, I thank you for doing so. I really hope that you enjoy all the riddles in this book. The riddles written in this book are great for children and adults alike no matter how old or what country you are from. By the time you finish, you will have joined in a common, popular pastime of many people. Riddles have been noted in historical documents all across the globe from China to India. The oldest recorded riddles are from Babylonian historical documents. Just like the Babylonians, you too can enjoy the benefits of riddles.

Some of the benefits of riddles are expected, and others are unexpected but just as beneficial. The first wonderful benefit of riddles is that they help you improve your vocabulary. When you encounter a word that you may not know, the riddle can help you use context clues to figure out the word. It will also expand your vocabulary and improve your reading comprehension as a result. The next amazing benefit of riddles is that they help you improve your logic and think faster. By trying to solve a riddle from every single angle, you improve your logic muscle. This helps problem-solving, which is an important trait in adulthood which can be gained just by solving funny riddles!

For younger people, riddles have shown to help increase their standardized test scores as well as improve intellectual humor. Riddles help young people develop a love for laughter that will help sustain them throughout the rest of their life. For the young at heart, riddles have shown to help prevent the risk of dementia and to improve memory. One of the most important benefits of riddles is that the problem-solving process releases a neurotransmitter called dopamine. Dopamine is important because it improves memory, concentration, understanding,, and positive thinking. Dopamine is the reason that you get a special thrill when you answer a riddle correctly and why you always want to try and figure out the riddle no matter if you know the answer or not. So, enjoy the dopamine release and have fun solving riddles. If you have somewhere to go, try not to lose track of time!

The King of Riddles book is divided into four different types of riddles. The first section of riddles is dedicated to easy "What Am I?" riddles followed by a section dedicated to hard "What Am I?" riddles. The last two sections are shorter and cover less and more tricky riddles respectively. The last two chapters contain the answers using the same number as the riddles. To get the maximum use of your brain power, try to hold off on looking at the answers until you can't think of any possible answer. Don't be afraid to think outside the box because that can lead to a train of thought that can help you solve the problem. However, if you need to use the answers, the answers are there for you! Remember, riddles are for you to have fun, so have fun! Challenge yourself and others and stretch your brain! Trust us, your brain will thank you. If you feel like you are stumped, you can take a deep breath, walk away, and come back or you can even ask for help. Whatever you do, remember to have fun! You may even want to mark the trickiest riddles to try on your friends and family members.

There are plenty of books on this subject on the market, so thanks again for choosing this one! I do not take it for granted that you decided to purchase this book. Every effort was made to ensure it is full of as much useful information as possible. Please enjoy!

Chapter 1: Super Easy Riddles — "What Am I?"

1. Drier, Yet Wetter

The more it dries, the wetter it becomes. I can be big or small and used on the beach or at home. What am I?

2. 3 Miles Away

You may try to chase me, but no matter how close you may think you are, I am always about 3 miles away. I can be beautiful, and people like to take my picture. What am I?

3. Single Eye

I have a single eye, but I cannot see. If you touch me, you may just prick yourself. What am I?

4. Black Water

I go in the water black and come out red. I am a special treat for many people who love seafood. What am I?

5. Light as a Feather

The world's strongest man is not able to hold me for more than 300 seconds even though I am like a feather. Please guess what I am.

6. No Water and Cities

I have bodies of water but no water. I have towns and villages but no beings. I even contain long roads, without any cars. Small or big, I can cover the entire world. What am I?

7. Two Legs

I have two legs, but I cannot walk. I can come in different styles and sizes. What am I?

8. Just Like Bacon

Sizzling like scissors, made with a small egg, containing a long spine, without one leg in sight. Peeling like an onion but longer than a shoelace. I can fit in tiny holes. Guess what I am.

9. An Easy Search

I am easy to get into but can be extremely hard to get out of. Some people love me, other people hate me. What am I?

10. Clap and Rumble

I can clap and rumble without any hands. I am loud and sometimes can be scary, but if you hear me, you know the earth will thank me. What am I?

11. Neck and No Head

Neck. Check. No head. Check. Can wear a cap. Check.
You need something special to open me. Figure me out.

12. Big Bark

Big bark. No bite. I exist in different species, but without
me, you would experience a certain death. Can you tell me
what I am?

13. Smooth or Rough Jacket

I can wear a smooth or rough jacket, but I don't wear any
pants. You can open me or close me, but many people see
my value. What am I?

14. Up and Down

I am in some of the most famous places in the world all
throughout history. I am in some people's house. Down
and up I go while being stationary. Please tell me what I
am.

15. Fly All Day

Lots of countries have me so I exist in a lot of different
colors and sizes. I fly all day, but I stay still like a couch
potato. Guess what I am if you can.

16. Wet Coat

   I am the type of coat that you can only put on when I am
   wet. You can put on multiple coats and not get hot. Some
   people even put up a sign to mark my spot. What am I?

17. Unwinnable Bet

   If you are a better, you might not like me because I am the
   type of bet that can never be won. I consist of many parts
   and even have my own song. What am I?

18. Unwearable Dress

   A snail has me on my back, but I am the type of dress that
   you cannot wear. Men and women both have me, old and
   young too. Sometimes ghosts live here and living beings
   too. What am I?

19. Eyes That Cannot See

   Blind eyes, a non-functional tongue, and an immortal soul I
   have. Some people see me in the clouds in the sky. What
   am I?

20. Serve, But Not Eaten

   You can serve me, but you cannot eat me. Some people
   love me, and others hate me. I am small, fast, and green.
   What am I?

21. Limbs But Cannot Walk

   I exist all over the world. I have over 100 limbs, but I
   cannot walk. Animals love to play on me and kids too.
   What am I?

22. Come Down, But Not Up

I can drizzle or pour. If you see me, some people want a jacket before they go out their home's door. Always coming down, I stay down and never return up. Are you smart enough to figure me out?

23. Beat with No Cries

I am white and yellow, the color of light. When you crack me, I will be alright. I get beaten and whipped but never cry. What am I?

24. Travel in One Spot

I consist of many different spaces, some living and some dead. Sometimes I just may be a shape or color, but you need me in order for a letter to be read. Visiting places in the world while remaining in one place, especially the corner. What am I?

25. Catch

I am one of the most feared things in the winter, and even in the summer. You can catch me but cannot throw me. People who have me can sometimes say, "Achoo." What am I?

26. Four Eyes

I look like a square and even have a delta. I have four eyes, but I cannot see. I am the spot of a lot of history. What am I?

27. Eighty-eight keys

I have eighty-eight keys but can't unlock anything. While tinkling and banging, musicians love to hear my name. What am I?

28. Always Coming

I am not the present, but I am being looked forward to. I am always coming, but I never arrive. Some people have their day planned weeks in advance. What am I?

29. Careful, Fragile

Some people love to make me, and sometimes people hate to make me. I get broken without being held. What am I?

30. Round on Both Sides

I am circular on the ends but reach the highest heights in the middle, all while being an important consideration in the politics of the United States of America. What am I?

31. Lose My Head

I am soft, and sometimes I am hard. I lose my head every morning, but it returns to me every night. Sometimes I am made of cotton, and sometimes I am made of feathers. People love to have me in any weather. What am I?

32. Hear, But No Body

I can be loud, or I can be soft. If you have me, you take me for granted. If you don't have me, you wish that you did. If you have ears, you can hear, but if you have fingers, you can't touch me or see me if you have eyes. What am I?

33. Poor and Rich People

There are a lot of people who get mad if they get me as a gift. Poor people have too much of it, but rich people supposedly will benefit from more of me. Eating me is a sure cause of death. Tell me what I am.

34. No Sharing

   There is something unique about me. I am special and only
   a few people should know about me. If I share me, there's
   no point, and if you have me, no sharing, please. Can you
   figure out what I am?

35. The More You Take

   I can be big or small, but you will need me at some point in
   your life. The more you take away, the larger I become.
   Some animals like to call me their home. What am I?

36. Born in the Air

   If you are quiet, I am no longer there. I live with no body,
   experience audio with no ears, and verbalize with no
   mouth. Oh yeah, I'm birthed in the air. What am I?

37. Millions of Years

   I can be white or orange and big or small. I have been here
   since the beginning of time but caught in an unending cycle
   of being born every month. What am I?

38. Give It Away

   I am a very important part of life. You can keep it only
   after giving it away to someone else. What is it?

39. Stand on One Leg

   Some people love me, and some people hate me, but if you
   eat me, you should never be dead. Standing straight on one
   leg with my heart in the same place as my head. Are you
   able to tell me what I am?

40. You Can Throw Me Away

   Squirrels and cows love me. I can be boiled or cooked on the grill. Trash me outside, prepare my innards, and trash my insides when you are finished. Guess what I am.

41. Used for Light

   I'm useful for light and solid. No me, and you would feel trapped, but I do not want to be touched. And don't even think of using force. I love being in buildings, and ancient I am if I must say. Most of us use me every day. What am I?

42. Higher Without the Head

   I am higher without the head than with it. What am I?

43. If I Drink

   I can be loud but start off soft. If you aren't listening, I can be fatal. Partaking of a beverage will cause my death, but partaking in a meal is not dangerous for me. What would you say that I am?

44. Take Away My First Letter

When you erase my first letter, last letter, and middle letter, I still sound the same. I am a five-letter word. What am I?

45. No Bones or Legs

I don't know if it was me or this animal that came first. While I have no legs or bones, if you give me a little heat, I can hurry away. What am I?

46. Tall When Young

My youth equals height and my age equals shortness. I can age fast or slow. If you have no electricity, you'll need me wherever you may go. What am I?

47. Throw Me Away

Pirates love me, and some people have me in their homes. Get rid of me when you want me to be useful. But if you want me to do nothing, bring me back in. What am I?

48. When Water Comes

The water pours, and I appear. The water pours, and I point to the sky. Some people use me to block the very bright sun. What am I?

49. The Maker Doesn't Need Me

If you make me, you will not need me at the moment. If you buy me, you don't even need me for yourself, but if you have to use me, you will never know. What am I?

50. People Need Me to Eat

You often can't have a meal unless you have me because I make your life easy. You need me at mealtime, but I'm not edible. Well, you can, but it wouldn't be very good. What am I?

51. Many Times

You can see me in the snow, and if you need to mark your spot without a compass, I am the way to go. The more you move, the more I trail you. Guess what I am.

52. End of the Rainbow

I am at the end of the colorful rainbow. It doesn't matter how big or small the rainbow is. What am I?

53. Never Ask Questions

I can be musical or just a simple sound. In front of a mansion, I will most likely be found. Questions you will never hear from me, but I get the answers I want. Tell me what I am.

54. No Life

I can be inside or outside. I can be used on lots of different devices. I may be in the background, but you will want to pay attention. Lifeless, I can die. If you don't have me, people can go berserk. I'm sure you know what I am.

55. A Speechless Mouth

With my mouth, I never shout. I can gurgle and murmur without ever stopping. I always jog, more like run, even without any legs. Guess what thing I am.

56. Lots of Memories

Memories are the only things I have because I have no material possessions. I house memories from years ago or from yesterday or today or even this very moment. What am I?

57. I Go Around and Around

I go around all the places in a city, town, and village, but I never can come inside. You will notice if I am not there, but if I am there, you hardly notice me. What am I, please?

58. Flying Without Wings

Wingless, I can fly fast or slow. When floating, I can be different colors. Eyeless, I can shed tears. What am I?

59. No Senses, But I Can Sense

I can experience the senses of sight, hearing, smelling, and taste with no tongue, notes, ears, or eyes. Some people may eat me, but you would not want to be around them. What am I?

60. Wrong Word

Simply put, pronouncing me correctly, you will always be wrong. Saying my name the right way, you are correct. Tell me what I am but try not to be wrong.

61. Locks and Unlocks

Even though I consist of keys, I have no locks. I may have space, but I have no room. Enter me, and you may escape, but you can't go outside. Can you guess what I am?

62. You Take Me

I am transported from a mine and encapsulated in a wooden case. While I cannot escape, being used worldwide is my thing. What am I?

63. Backwards Cheese

I am a cheese made in the reverse. Please tell me what I am.

64. Lots of Letters

I am a building that ends in the letter 'e' and starts with the letter 'p.' I may be small or large, but either size, I store thousands of letters, too. What am I?

65. A Type of Ship

I am a ship that has two mates but no captains in sight. What am I?

66. A Mini Tree

Even though I am a tree, you can fit me in your hand. Are you smart enough to tell me what I am?

67. Super Delicate

I am something that is very fragile and delicate. You have to listen to avoid breaking me. Speak my name and I am of no use. Tell me what I am.

68. One Head, not Human

I have one head, but I am not human. I have one foot and four legs. I may sound like a freak, but people are hardly scared of me. What am I?

69. Everyone Needs Me

Everyone in the world needs me. If more people used me, the world would be a better place. People always give me, but people hardly ever take me. I am cheaper than going to a therapist. What am I?

70. What Word

I am a word. When you add two letters to me, I get shorter. If you don't pay attention, I'm gone. May you tell me what I am?

71. A Vehicle

Now you see me. Briefly. Now you don't. Too bad. A type of vehicle, I am spelled the exact same way forwards and backwards. What am I?

72. What State

I am small yet popular. If you come here, you will never forget. I am a state that is surrounded by a lot of water and a place to come if you are ever upset. What am I?

73. Every Night

I come out every night without having to be called. I can twinkle or be dim. However, I can disappear just like I appear. I am lost every day without being stolen. What am I?

74. Center of Gravity

Don't overlook me, but you can if you're are not looking too closely. I am at the center of gravity. Without me, there is no such thing as gravity. Tell me what I am if you dare.

75. A Fruit

I am a fruit. If you take away my first letter, you will get a body part. If you take away the initial and last letter, a video game company I am. Do you know what I am?

76. No Flaky Hair

With ear, I am deaf. Having flakes, I am hairless. Can you take the challenge? Please explain what I am.

77. Pilgrim Music

I was the type of music that the early Pilgrims loved to listen to. What am I?

78. Dangerous

I can hurt you without moving an inch. I can poison you without touching you. I can tell the truth, and I can also lie. Size isn't a factor. Please say what I am.

79. A Man's Weakness

I weaken all men for hours each day. I show you weird visions while you are away. I take you by night, by day, I take you back. None suffer from having a lot of me, but they suffer from not having enough of me. What am I?

80. I Belong to You

I technically may be yours, but others may feel more inclined to it. Are you capable of telling me what I am?

81. I Can Be

Short. Long. Grown or used because I'm your own. Painted or blank. Square, coffin or stiletto. What I am depends on your guess.

82. I Have Just One

One for sure. Eight others to spare. Typically, I'm nice, but other times I'm ambivalent. Please guess what I am.

83. Men Hear Me

At the sound of me, loud or soft, men dream and move their feet. My sound, loud and or soft, causes men to cry or giggle. Will you be able to tell me what I am?

84. No Hinges

No hinges, screws, keys, or lock, yet a precious treasure is inside. Tell me what I am.

85. A Single Color

A single color but a multitude of colors. I may be at the bottom, but I can fly. You see me in the sun, and I disappear in the rain. Harmless and painless, can you tell me what I am?

86. Reach for the Sky

I may be gone if you don't pay attention, but I'm in the background. I strive for the sky, but I'm still around. What am I?

87. Three Letters

With just three letters, I am the same going the front way and going the back way. Tell me what word I am.

88. Sometimes white, sometimes black,

sometimes I am the brightest of whites, but most of the time, I am the darkest of blacks. I will take you there, but you will never come back. Traffic stops because of me, and I am often an overlooked part in people's history. What am I?

89. Green, red, or other

Sometimes red, sometimes green, and sometimes our color is in between. Some spray us. I can be hot or cold, but don't touch your eyes after touching me. What am I?

90. Many Legs

I may have lots of legs, but I am unable to stand. A long neck I have, but no head. Unable to walk and unable to see, I still keep things tidy. Tell me what I am, please.

91. An Insect

While I'm an insect, there is another insect within the first part of my name. A famous group even has a name like mine. Don't squash me when you see me. Please tell me what I am.

92. Many Feathers

Feathers help me soar, but it's up to you to tell me the distance I can go. I, not alive, but I have a head. Can you guess what I am?

93. The Tool of a Potato

The potato loves to use me because I am powerful. I can be used every 60 or 30 minutes. If my cells are gone, I am no longer a working tool. Tell me what I am if you dare.

94. No Lungs

I don't have any legs to tango, waltz, or do the polka. I am even lungless. I can dance and breathe even though I am not alive. Are you able to decipher what I am?

95. First in the Ocean

My initial letter is in the opera, but never in sync. My second letter is in waffle, but never in beetle. My third letter is in gloat and also in fly, which is exactly what I do at night. I'm begging you. Please tell me what I am.

96. Very Skinny

Slim and introverted, I only live for about 60 minutes, and then I'm gone. In the hour I'm alive, I eat all I can. When people see me, they are not happy, but when I leave, they hate it. Are you able to guess what I am?

97. Invisible, Yet There

Unable to be touched, seen, or felt, I am in every single being. Some people argue if I am alive or not, but there is a genre of music that is my namesake. Please tell me what I am if you are smart enough.

98. Skinny and Lean

I am lean and skinny and many like that. You experience good feelings when you touch me, albeit, short-lived. I only shine once and then no more after that. Can you tell me what I am?

99. To Measure or to Not Measure

You won't know me until you measure me, but when I am flown, you will miss me because I'm gone. Are you smart? Are you capable? Can you figure me out? What am I?

100. White and Grind

White is my color. Cutting and grinding are my things, but if I am broken, you have to fill or remove me. I can be sharp or dull or real or fake. Whatever it is, you'll want me when you're eating steak. What am I?

101. Walk on Four Legs

Four. Two. Three. This explains how many legs I walk on at the beginning, middle, and end of my life respectively. What am I?

102. Cannot Control Me

Humans make me, but they have no power on me. I suck on different things like flesh or paper and sometimes all at the same time. I can be more harmful than helpful at times. I am a tornado of energy and can be everywhere all the time. Tell me what I am if you can.

103. Try and Catch Me

I am everywhere, but not seen. I am captured, but not helped. I have no throat to speak, but you will hear me. Are you able to figure out what I am about? Can you tell me what I am?

104. One Blind Eye

I only have one eye, but it is not used to see. I may enjoy the ocean, but I am unable to have fun and swim in it. I am white on my back and gray on my stomach. I may come, but I don't stay too long. Can you tell me what I am, please?

105. Different Colors

When you first get me, I am black. When you put me to use, I turn red. And I transform into white when you're all done with me. Some people love me, but if you use me without asking it could end in disaster. What am I?

106. Pointed Teeth

My pointy teeth wait for my next victim. When I got you, you will know, you'll feel my bite from head to toe. My victims normally don't have any blood, but you sure wouldn't want me to bite you. Are you able to figure out what I am?

107. No Eyes

I don't have an eye now, but I used to be able to see. I once had thoughts, but I am now empty. I used to be full of vim, but not I am lean and trim. What am I?

108. Weight in My Belly

I can be heavy because I have a solid stomach, and my back is made of trees. Nails pierce my ribs, but I don't have any feet. Doesn't matter how much weight I carry, I'll get it done, whether fast or slow. What am I?

109. Cannot Be Seen

You can't see me. You can't hear me. You can't smell me. I reside behind the balls in the sky and hide before hills. I always fill in the holes that are empty. I exist first and then after that. I stop life and the joy of laughter. I am tricky, I know. Can you tell me what I am?

110. Light and Hidden

I am made of something but lighter than that. Most of me is hidden, but you'll still want to be careful. Care to tell me what I am?

111. Between Your Head and Toes

Toes and head are what you use me in between. The more you use me, the smaller I get. What am I?

112. Different Sizes and Shapes

Straight or curves, patterns and shapes are many that I come in. I go wherever you want, but there is only one way I truly go. Are you able to tell me the thing that I am?

113. Sleep Throughout the Day

Unlike you, I sleep in the day, and I fly in the darker day without having any feathers. Tell me what I am if you can.

114. Travel Low and High

I go low and I go high. You can find me between any line if you read them. If there is no me, there is no sound in the world. Please tell me what I am.

115. None Seeps

Liquid can get on me, but I will not get wet. If you hit me, I am like a chameleon and can change colors. I cover lots of things, I'm quite complex. Can you tell me what I am?

116. Thirty Men

Thirty men and two ladies are what I consist of. We just stand around. Still, we look great. However, if we move about, a fight will break out. Are you able to tell me what I am?

117. Often Held

You can hold me without touching me. I can't rust even though I am perpetually wet. I can bite but more rarely bitten. Some have me but can't use me. I may be guessed if you are smart.

118. Up and Down

I can go down and up simultaneously. I am both the present and the past tense. Are you ready to go for a ride? What word I am is up to you.

119. Tear Me Off

You can rip me and put scratches on my noggin. I'm black now even though I used to be red. Careful, careful, try not to singe a finger or you will have one painful member. What am I?

120. Fingers—Nope

I don't have any fingers, but I have two arms. I cannot run, but I have two feet. I can carry things the best when my feet are off the ground. Please tell me what I am if you can.

121. Crack a Smile

I prefer smiles over frowns. But whatever you give me, I'll adjust automatically. When you drop me, I often crack. However, if you give me a lovely smile, right back at you, I'll give the smile back. Are you able to tell me what thing I am?

122. Always Old

I am always old, but sometimes I am new. I can be blue but never sad. I am sometimes full but never empty. I do not push, but I always pull. What am I?

123. Loud Noise

Watch out. Switching out my jacket will cause a huge sound. I weigh less even though I look larger. Are you able to tell me what I am?

124. You Hear

You heard me before, and you'll hear me again. Then I will die until you call me again. What am I?

125. What Letter

Rock I am, but I am not stone. In marrow, you can find me but not in bone. Find me in the bolster, but you will not find me in bed. Nowhere in living, and I am not in the dead. What am I?

126. Ruler of Shovels

There may not be many people who want to be a ruler of shovels, but I do, and I love my job. For some people, I am the end goal. I am one of a double and thin like a knife blade. Oh yeah, I have a wife. Tell me what I am.

127. Fingers Equal Four

No blood and no flesh, but I have a thumb and fingers that equal four. Are you able to tell me what the thing is that I am?

128. The Pope Does Not Use It

He does not use it, but the Pope has it. Your mom uses it just like your dad. The husband of your girlfriend has it, and she also uses it. Do you know what I am?

129. Invisible Roots

The roots I have are invisible. The trees are not as tall as me, but I do not grow. You're a genius if you can tell me what I am.

130. Nothing on the Outside

On the inside and on the outside, there is nothing. Twenty men can't lift me, although I am lighter than paper. What am I?

131. Beauty in the Sky

Beautiful and magical all throughout the sky, I just can't fly. I'm good luck to some, and others think I bring them riches. Please tell me what I am.

132. No Drinks from This

No one can drink me, and I am a fountain. For people who search me, I am like gold. However, the more I continually die, I bring riches to everyone who wants more. Tell me what I am if you can, please.

133. A Precious Stone

Clear like a diamond, I am considered a precious stone. Find me when the sun is close to the horizon. My power helps you walk on water, but if you keep me, I will be gone in an hour. Are you able to tell me what I am?

134. A Beamer

Beaming, shining, sparkling white, the day becomes brighter when I am around from a single light. Enchanting and charming, that's what I do to all. Bringing out the best in you is what I do to you all. Can you please tell me what I am?

135. I Devour

Flowers, beasts, birds, and trees are all the things that I devour. Really, I devour everything. I eat iron and steel easily and make hard stones dust. I kill famous men and cause mountains to go down, plus I ruin towns. What am I?

136. I Am Small

Tiny, but bigger than a bee, I am nimble like a flea, except I don't buzz. I hum my songs. I love delectable flower nectar. What am I?

137. I Am Big

Huge and bulky, my long trunk is like a tree. I keep water in my nose which is like a hose. What am I?

138. I March Before Armies

I am ahead of armies and people love to give me their attention. If I fall, it's over but not because I've been killed. I love the wind, and the wind loves my non-legged self. What am I if you can guess?

139. Beginning of Ideas

You don't think of me, but I am an important part of history. I am at the beginning of lots of good ideas. But if you don't like your idea, crumble and toss me out. Tell me what I am.

140. My Children

Near and far is where my children are, but I can always find them. I give them gifts to make them happy, but if I leave, my children are going away. Can you tell me what I am?

141. I Can Fall

If I fall off a skyscraper, I will be okay, but if I fall into the water, it's a quick, slow death. What am I?

142. Can You See

If you pause and observe, you can see me. If you try to feel me, you are not able to. If you come close to me, I will move from you even though I can't move. Are you able to tell me what I am?

143. You Have Me

You have me today. Tomorrow, you'll have more. As your time passes, I'm not easy to store. I don't take up space, but I am only in one place. I am what you saw but now what you see. What am I?

144. In You

I am always in you and sometimes on you. If I surround you, I can kill you. I hope you can figure me out.

145. Cracked

Cracked, told, played, and made are all things that I can do. Please guess what I am.

146. I Am Red

I am red, blood pumps through me, and I live throughout your physical body. Love is what I realize. Can you tell me what I am if you don't mind?

147. Sweet Rest

You can use me when you're resting. I am soft and comfortable, and I protect your neck and head. You can ask for me on an airplane, and fighting with me can be fun. What am I?

148. Soup or Burger

You can find me in soup or on a hamburger. When raw, I am green, but when ripened, I am red and becomes a savory condiment. What am I?

149. Children Love Me

Children love to play with me, but not inside, only out. Watch out for the wires and trees for you could tangle me. Look up and watch me dance. The faster you run, the faster I will wiggle. What am I?

150. The Ocean Is My Home

The ocean is my real home. It is common you find me in red, pink, blue, or gold. Humans trick me into biting. My favorite thing is blowing bubbles, and if you take me home with you, I will be an easy pet to take care of. What am I?

151. Don't Drop Me

I can connect you to the world even though sometimes you ignore me. I am covered with buttons, and my sounds can be unique. Don't drop me, or I might crack. What am I?

152. I Wiggle

I can't see, but I wiggle. On a tree, you can find me, which I prefer over being on a hook. Even if you don't realize it, sometimes I am in a book. Are you able to tell me what I am if you are good enough to figure it out?

153. The Special Room

You can't come in, even though I am a room. Sometimes I am poisonous, and sometimes I am delicious to eat. What am I?

154. Wave Me

Waving my hands is a symbol of leaving even though I cannot actually say good-bye. Use me when you're hot, and I will cool you off. What am I?

155. Three Eyes

One leg. Three eyes. Listen to me, or you might get into trouble. What am I?

156. Forward and Backward

Forward and backwards, I go every day. Different sizes, colors, and shapes are what I come in. Some I might fright, but for most, they go night-night. What am I?

157. Long Tail

My tail is long. My coat can be black or grey. I live in the house of which I live outside. I come out to have fun when you are in dreamland. Please tell me what I am.

158. Carry Me

Carry me with you, and I will keep your hair dry. Short or long I can be, opened or closed. I'm not a problem unless you use me in the house. What am I?

159. No Voice

I teach you with no voice. No spines or hinges I have, not even a door. I tell you what you need to know, then I go. Are you able to tell me what I am?

160. Different Colors

Many beautiful different colors are what I come in. I smell nice, and you can pick me up if you want. I will live for a long time as long as you water me. Guess what you can to tell me what I am.

161. Bigger When Full

There are many different colors that I come in. I will float away if you don't tie me down, and I will make a loud sound if I break. What am I?

162. Brick Body

My body is usually made of brick or wood, and I come with a lot of windows and doors. Keep me clean for visitors, and I will keep you warm and cozy. You can sell me if your family grows. What am I?

163. Keep Me Away

I am the enemy of paper, and small children shouldn't be around me. Create me when you're doing art or when you're doing your hair. Tell me what I am.

164. Easily Overlooked

No one pays attention to me even though we all have one. If you can, are you able to tell me what I am?

165. The Harder You Run

You can run very hard, but it will be more difficult for you to capture me. Please tell me what I am.

166. Twirl My Body

Twirling my body is what I do, but I keep my head very high. Once I'm in, it's very difficult to remove me. Guess what I am.

167. A Seed

I have three letters in my name and with all three, I am a type of see. When you take away the last two letters, I still sound the same. Try and figure me out.

168. Going Up

Up and up I go, and I don't come down. As I go higher, my wrinkle count goes up too. Can you please tell me what I am?

169. Green Jacket

I am a green, white, and red sandwich with lots of black sprinkled throughout. Are you able to figure me out?

170. Black as Night

I'm very dark, and I have three eyes. I can knock down 10 in one go. Please tell me if you are able to guess me.

171. Good at Hiding

I help you be courageous, but I hide the truth. If you can figure me out, you're great.

172. Pure, But Forgotten

I can be rotten every now and then, but I am always around you although you forget. Tell me what I am.

173. Run

You combine my bodies together, and when I am not moving, I run. Are you able to tell me what thing I am?

174. A Mother

My kids are equal to the number eight, and I turn all day even though I have weight. There was a ninth kid before I realized it was fake. Can you tell me what I am?

175. Never Stolen

I am unable to be taken from because I am collectively owned, although some people have less, and some have more. Can you please guess what I am?

176. Enjoyed by Some

I will be here forever unless you get rid of me. Some people love me, and others hate me, but I'm not that bad if you do it right. What am I?

177. Soft and Hairy

Sort, hairy, and I stretch from door to door. I'm always on the floor. Tell me what I am. I know you can.

178. A Ring

No fingers, but a ring I have. Typically, I am still, but now I can follow you wherever you go. Tell me what I am.

179. Take Off My Clothes

Your clothes go, mine come on. My clothes come on, your clothes go. I know you can do it. Please tell me what I am.

180. Metal or Bone

You may want me to bite you because my bite does not hurt. Wood, metal, or bone are my ingredients. Are you able to figure out what this is about?

181. Run Around

Back and forth, I go throughout the day, but I rest when I'm done. I'm so tired that my tongue is out at the end of the day. Can you tell me what I am?

182. The Protector

I protect people. That's what I do. Sitting on a bridge is what I do even though people can see straight through me. Some people want to know what's underneath. Can you figure me out?

183. An Absolute Necessity

Some people need me, and they love me when among family and friends. I can be hot or cold but enjoyable for all, doesn't matter if it's light or dark. When you finish drinking me, I leave my mark. Are you able to tell me what I am?

184. Not Born

I am here even though I am not birthed. I have lots of names, but I am not given an official name and birthed by life and science. Figure me out if you can.

185. In the Rainforest

Everywhere you go, you may not find me. But if you are in a rainforest, you will see me with my weird number of toes. I'm probably chilling upside down and very lazy. See if you can figure me out.

186. Buttons or a Zipper

I have buttons or a zipper, pockets or sometimes a belt. I'll protect you from a cold wind, but you won't need me in the summer. When you are done with me, please hang me in the closest. What am I?

187. Jump and Climb

I can jump, and I can climb. With my many legs, I swing from tree to tree. I can make a house much bigger than me. What am I?

188. Go Up

I am round. Up and down, I go. Catching and throwing me is what you can do, but use caution near windows. Figure me out.

189. Keep You Entertained

I will keep you entertained with my drama and my comedy. I am shaped like a cube, and I can attach to your wall. What am I?

190. Curly and Bald

You can call me curly, and you can call me bald. You can call me gray, you can call me shaggy. Long or short is what I can be. Tell me what I am, please.

191. In the Woods

In the woods is where you got me. When you sat down is when you found me. And it hurts, but it's okay. Please tell me what I am.

192. Wake You

I can wake you in the morning without electricity, batteries, or winding. What am I?

193. Lick, Lick

I am a delicious treat that you can lick with your tongue. I come in a cone or in a bowl. One of my common flavors is also a common scent. What am I?

194. Fruit

Good taste and lots of energy are what I give when you eat me. I may be your favorite fruit. Single people can like me. You can also find me in a calendar in lots of boxes. What am I?

195. Two Meanings

Two meanings are what I hold. One is broken, and the other holds on. Are you able to tell me what I am?

196. A Food

Five letters are what I have. When you take away the first letter, I give you energy. Take away the first two letters, and I am necessary to life. Take away the last three letters, and you can drink me. Have at it. Figure out what I am.

197. I Am Scary

I exit your ears and cause fear in others. I am quiet, like mice, but no one wants me in their house. Can you tell me what I am?

198. A Small Piece of Paper

Small yet valuable, I am only a piece of paper. You need me for big events and travel. Tell me what I am.

199. Can Be Embarrassing

Sometimes people get embarrassed when you stand on me and a whole lot of people watch. Women hate me and stand on me in secret. Can you tell me what I am?

200. People Walk in Me

Come and go inside of me. You push me, and I will do what you say. When you leave me, I wait for the next command and the next person to come into my life. Can you please tell me what I am?

Chapter 2: Super Hard Riddles — "What Am I?"

1. At the Beginning

   At the beginning of end, at the end of place. At the end of space and time, and at the beginning of place. Can you figure out what I am?

2. First in Bridge

   In bridge, but not ridge is my first letter. In awake, but not in mistake is my second letter. The third is not in ranger but in danger. The fourth letter is in gooey, but not in ooey. My fifth is in spine, and the last is in winter. Tell me what I am.

3. Creature of Power

   I am a creature of power and a creature of grace, a creature of beauty and a creature of strength. I set everything in the world's pace, for all things in the world must stay under my green influence. Can you please let me know what I am?

4. Sisters That Are Two

   We are sisters that are two. One is bright, and one is dark. We stay in twin homes, and people love us together. Who are we?

5. Four-Letter Word

I am a versatile word consisting of four letters. No matter how you read me, I am the same. Can you tell me what you think I am?

6. The Traveling Letter

I can move from over here to over there by going way and then come here to there by coming back again. What letter will you say that I am?

7. Covered in White

I cover the rolling hills in white. While I am not able to swallow, I can definitely bite. What am I?

8. White and Dirty

I am something that most people have come in contact with. I am difficult to clean because the whiter I am, the dirtier I get. What am I?

9. Hard Tongue

My tongue isn't soft, so you can really hear me speak. Since I'm lungless, I can't breathe. I can be loud or soft even though I don't have a voice. What am I?

10. Letters Equal to Six

This word means a group but erasing the first letter means wood that burns. Tell me what I am.

11. Three Lives

Three lives I have. Crack rocks, sooth skin, and hugging the sky are all things that I do. Can you please tell me what I am?

12. Sky and Ground

Ground and in the sky are where you can find me. I always end with an f. What am I?

13. Fall and Break

I fall, but I am unbreakable. Even if I break, I don't fall in order to do so. I am what two things?

14. Water of Life

I am the water of life but seeing too much of me is never good. I am what brings families together, but I can be defied. What am I?

15. Forward

When you see me forward, I weigh a ton. But when you see me backwards, I do not. Please tell me what I am.

16. Feel Me, But Can't See

Touch me, but you can't use your eyes to see me. You shiver when I come and are relieved when I pass. What am I?

17. With Me

Although I don't get wet, I am used in a bath. Tell me what I am if you can?

18. Red Tears

My tears are red when you squeeze, but I have a heart made of stone. What am I?

19. Use Me Everyday

You use me every day but let me rest at night. I have an exact twin with me all the time. And somehow, you always cover me up. I have a soul but not alive. What am I?

20. Creative Memories

You can hear me and feel me, but you can't see me or smell me, yet everyone has a taste in me. I can be created, but after that only remembered. What am I?

21. Served

Served in two or four, tiny, circular and white, I am fun when you see me at a table. Please let me know what I am.

22. Out from Earth

They sell me in the mart, and I come out from earth. When you purchase me, off my tail goes and my silk suit. But you cry when I am dead. Are you able to guess what I am?

23. Dog's Name

I am a dog's name consisting of only one letter and one number. What am I?

24. Straight Through Me

I move like lighting, so fast that you can't watch me. Everyone can see right through me, and I go forever, even until the day you die. Can you please let me know what I am?

25. Negative Magic

Magic I am, but reality I show. However, making your hand on the right, transform to your left, and your hand on the left transform into your right. Tell me what I am.

26. Share but Selfish

You can share me, but still have me all to yourself. What am I?

27. I Am Two

There is one in room, and in the corner, there are two, but shelter only has one. Can you tell me what I am?

28. Thunder Before Lightning

Thunder arrives in the moments before the lightning. The lightning comes in the moments before the rain, and rain makes all the ground dry that it touches. Are you capable of figuring me out?

29. Five and Six

Once you put six and five together, you get eleven, but when you take the numbers seven and six together, you get the number one. Can you guess what I am?

30. Give Me Away

People need me, some more than others, but they always give me away. You give me intentionally away for a gift or unintentionally for carelessness. What am I?

31. Starts with Gas

   I start with gas and have 10 letters. What am I?

32. Run Around

   I run all around the pasture, but I never move. I can be around your house, too. What am I?

33. Shave Beards

   I shave beards all day, but I still have a beard. Who am I?

34. Which Word

   This entire word means an awesome woman, but the first two letters mean a man, and the first three letters mean a woman, and the first four mean an awesome man. Which word am I?

35. Past Is the Past

   The past is where I stay. The present is where I'm made, but the future can't touch me. Are you able to guess what I am correctly?

36. See Me in Water

   The water is where you will find me, all dry of course. What am I?

37. My Brother

You see my brother, not me. You can hear me, but not him. Where I am, my brother is, too. What am I and who is my brother?

38. I Travel Alone

I travel alone, never lonely. My name is real, but I don't exist. What am I?

39. Summertime Favorite

Friends like to have me. I am not living, but I still grow. Oh yeah, I'm a summertime favorite. Can you figure me out?

40. Sweet or Sour

I'm not a rhyming word but have sweetness and some sour. Are you able to tell me what I am?

41. Compliments People

The digit that compliments people is my first. The second digit points to things. The digit to hurt people is my third one. The fourth digit may just hold a treasure, and fancy people love my fifth digit when they drink things. Are you capable of figuring out what I am?

42. A Circle

I'm essentially a circle, nothing really, but I'm worth tenfold. Are you able to tell me what I am?

43. Two in a Whole

I am two in a whole and four in a pair. Six in a trio you see. Eight's a quartet but what you must get is the name that fits just one of me. What am I?

44. Digging a Tiny Cave

Dig and dig is what I do, putting silver and gold where holes used to be. Tell me what I am if you can?

45. Simple or Complex

Shapes. Colors. Complex. Simple. I am all of that and found in daily life. Perhaps even in this riddle. Can you figure out what I am?

46. Some People

    Count, consume, avoid are all things that people do to me.
    Can you tell me what I am?

47. It May Sound

    It may sound as if I work in the transport industry, but I
    really work in fine dining. Do you know what I am?

48. Shimmery Field

    I am a far-reaching shimmery swatch of land without
    noticeable tracks but crossable. What am I?

49. Write on Me

    I keep secrets. You can write on me even though like a top
    I am because I spin. I can be used as a mop even though I
    can be used as a board, as well. You got it. See if you can
    let me know what I am.

50. Folding

Folding paper is how you can get me even if you do your best to avoid me. I'm small but painful. May you guess me?

51. Two Occupants

We live together two at a time, but sometimes you can squeeze in three. You eat my insides and throw my outsides away. What am I?

52. Walking and Running

When you walk, you know it's running. When I run, you know I'm walking. Are you able to figure out what I am?

53. Not My Name

My name is not my own and no one cares about me when they are on top. People shed tears when they see me and stay by my side night plus day. Tell me what I am if you can.

54. In Window

I'm white and very popular to have at a very popular event among people. Peaceful, I'm still a bird, bringing good news since the days of Noah. Will you tell me what I am?

55. You Can't Hide

You don't know when I am coming, but I am coming. Some expect me, and others don't. Just try to be ready when I arrive. Do you know what I am?

56. Brown Is What I Am

I smell like something purses are made of and you can put me on horses or on men. Tell me what I am, and you win this riddle.

57. The Path

You can use me as a path between things made by nature and as a path by things made by men. Can you tell me what I am?

58. Once a God

I used to be called a god, and for some people, I am still their angel. You either hate me or love me. Are you able to figure out what I am?

59. Soft Like Silk

   I am soft like a pillow, white a cloud, and puffy like a tutu.
   I am the nastiest part of the tool you use to clean the floor.
   Please figure me out if you can.

60. Two-Faced

   Two-faced and many people have fought over me. I may
   be small, but you wished that you had me every time you
   go through a toll or need to use a parking meter. Tell me
   what I am if you can.

61. Very Tempting

   My coat can be smooth or pock-marked, yellow, green, or
   red. My insides are sweet and can be sweet or sour. You
   should love to pick me because I can save you a trip to the
   doctor. In some circles, I'm considered a temptation. Can
   you figure me out?

62. Young and Great

   I am more valuable when I am older than when I am
   younger. Stepping on me may seem crazy, but it's the best
   thing to do. If you keep me long enough, you may have a
   small inheritance. Are you smart enough to figure out what
   I am?

63. My Title

   I have pages, but I'm not a book. I have a title, but I'm not
   a book. I am a killer and slave, but I'm still not a book. Try
   to tell me what I am if you can.

64. Head Bob

I'm a head bobber with white hair and a cutesy yellow face. By the way, most of my body is green. Can you guess what I am?

65. Head or Tail

Head or tail, I'm perfect either way. Can you tell me what I am?

66. Add the Letter 'S'

Most people add the letter 's' to a word to make it mean more than one. But I'm special. I am a word that becomes plural when you add the letter 'C' instead. What am I?

67. More Shoes

Most of the shoes I have equal more than what anybody else can have. However, I have no feet. In the morning, you see me, but at night, I'm gone. I will shake when I am angry, but I am not going to bite. Are you able to tell me what I am?

68. Your Mechanic's Name

I am a mechanic's name. When your physical life is over, I may just have all your wealth. Can you get it? Can you figure out? Can you tell me what I am?

69. Beneath Your Roof

I live with you while you are alive, and I can live with you while you die. You need me to pay taxes, and you need me to write. Please guess what I am.

70. Evil Cutter

I fight for right, and I cut through evil just like butter. Not too far to the right and not too far to the left, I am all about being fair. Guess me if you can.

71. I Have Two

Two things I have, so you can have one, and I can have one. If you ask me about the price, I just nod my head and give you a smile. What can I be?

72. Want a Sweet

When craving sweetness, I am the place that you should come. If you can't stand the heat, then you need to get out. Are you able to tell me what I am?

73. Busy, Busy

On many busy streets, you will find me. If you keep me fed, you will be happy. But if you make me hungry, you're going to hate me. Please tell me what I am.

74. I Heard of a Wonder

I am an interesting person, half animal, half-human, all intelligence. You will see me in a coffee shop or library near you. But you may overlook me if you didn't have this clue. Can you tell me what I am?

75. Moving Slow

I am extremely slow moving, but if you want me to go faster, you can find assistance in the store. I am everywhere on some people and on others I'm sparer, but if you have none, you'll wish I was there. Explain what I am if you dare.

76. Take a Spin

Take me for a spin, and I'll make you cool, but use me in the winter, and you're a big fool. What am I?

77. Bury Me

Interestingly, when I am alive, you put me in the ground, but you dig me up when there is no more life in my body. Can you figure me out?

78. I Can Help You See

Castle-builder, mountain-destroyer, man-blinder, but sometimes I can help men see. Guess what I am.

79. Born of Water

I am born of water, and I drown in water. I am a blood-thirsty beast that you can barely see. What am I?

80. You Will Face Me

Face me and be happy. Most young people love me, although, older people tend to dislike me. Even if you forget me, that will not stop me from happening. Tell me what I am, please, if you can.

81. Silver-tongued

I am teary-eyed but never once dropped a tear. I am silver-tongued but never lived. I am double-winged but never fly, and I am air-cooled but never dry. What am I?

82. Twelve Is Left

I have six total letters, but when you just take one of those letters away, twelve is actually left. Can you make this math makes sense? Please tell me what I am.

83. White Father, Black Child

I am black, but my dad is white. I don't have any wings, but I fly to the heavens. When you meet me, you may cry, even though there is no reason to cry. However, at my birth, I go back into thin air. Are you able to tell me what I am?

84. Alive Without a Breath

Chilly like death, alive without having to breathe, I always drink, so my thirst is always quenched. Figure me out if you can.

85. Visible to You

If I am there, you are not able to see me. When I am away, you will wish to be assured of my presence. If you are slow and thoughtful, I am in abundance. But if you are fast and rash, I am hardly around. Are you able to tell me what I am?

86. Speak the Truth

I speak to you without talking. Everything in it is a lie, but that doesn't stop you from believing it. I am the source of countless joy of many across the world. Just suspend your disbelief. What am I?

87. Creatures of the Air

We are creatures of speech, yet everyone needs us no matter what language you speak. We are only five, but we are powerful. Without us, there would be a whole lot less words. Think really hard but not too deep. Soon enough, you'll find the answer that you seek.

88. Peep, Peep

My sister is young, and she does a double peep. She goes throughout the waters very deep. She climbs as high as she can on the mountains, but unfortunately, she only has one eye socket. Who can I be?

89. Utensil Love

Bread or a paper cutter is what I am being used for. Thugs or wives use me, one for nefarious means and the other for means not so nefarious. What am I?

90. A Hundred Years

I have been here for over one hundred years. I give food and find food on my own consisting of rain and sun to name a few. I don't move much, but when I do, you will be able to use me for other things. If you think long and hard, you can figure me out. What do you think I am?

91. Helping Engines

Pants or engines, I help both of them function. Think, and you can figure me out.

92. They Belong to Me

I am mine, and I am yours. I can make you feel all types of emotions from yellow to blue. I will keep going until the day that you do not go any more. Figure me out, and tell me what I am.

93. Round Am I

Similar to a round chess-board, I can be curled and whirled. Some play me personally or watch me from their home, but anyone can play me if they want to bad enough. What am I?

94. Beautiful and Cold

Cold and beautiful, old, and young, alive, and always dead. When you feed me, I'm still hungry. I can die if I bleed enough or if you chop my head off. Can you figure out what I am?

95. Lovely and Round

I am round and lovely, shining with a pale light, brought up in the dark, the joy of many women. Please tell me what I am if you can.

96. End of My Yard

Twenty-four women are dancing in my year in green gowns and blue hats. Tell me what I am if you can.

97. Makes No Sense

I make absolutely no sense. If you are in me, you will either fall hard or fly high. I make you do everything because my need is a necessity of biology but an illogical anomaly. I'm not real, but if you work hard, you can achieve them if you believe in yourself. What am I?

98. First a Blessing

I was a blessing sent to earth after the flowers and plants were nourished. Then I was sent as a reminder for hope, and I'm not too bad on the eyes. If you guess me, I will be surprised. Can you tell me what I am?

99. Used for Light

While solid, I am used for light. If I am not around, you will feel trapped. I do not like to be touched. Oh yeah, I enjoy being in buildings. Say ye, what I am?

100. Backbite

I rarely walk even though I have lefts. I will never speak, but I will backbite. I look for places that can hide me. What am I you say? You tell me.

101. I Can Wave

I will wave at you, but it's not to say goodbye. When I am up high, you are especially cool with me. Can you figure out what I am?

102. Forest Without Trees

Similar to a forest without trees is what I am. Similar to a jail you want to visit because the inmates are innocent. Don't feed the inmates, and you can walk wherever you want to. What am I?

103. Heavy Feet

People have heavy feet when they come to visit me. I hold one, and when I am able to, I will dance, turn, and spin. What do you think I am? What can I possibly be?

104. Day Sleeping

I hide and sleep through the day because I am up all night. I shine briefly in comparison to when I sleep. Watch out or you will miss me. Can you guess the right answer to what I am?

105. Lacking Reason

I rhyme but don't make much sense. That's why you need logic as one of my requirements. The words you need for your kinfolk or your friends are there if you look within. By the way, the answer is basically in my name. Can you tell me what I am?

106. I Drink

I am more poisonous than the venom found in snakes. Quietly, I drink in fluids that are darker than the night. I beat the mightiest of warriors but not in a fight. Can you figure out what I am?

107. A Tradition

Once upon a long time ago, I used to be a very important tradition during the dark ages. Men did magical things like transforming the dark into the light and by mixing magic potions, supposedly in the night. Unfortunately, the efforts didn't work because they were burned as witches. What tradition would you say that I am?

108. Small and Light

Even though I am small, I am full of light. Don't forget me because you need me to shine in the night. I can help light up whatever pyre you want because I am able to start fires. What am I?

109. Four Total Legs

I don't have an ounce of hair, but I have a total of four whole legs. I am always ready to work even though people ride me for hours. I don't go anywhere without you giving me a nudge. What would you say that I am?

110. Daily Dawn

Daybreak and dawn could not happen without me at all. Daisies also grow from me, and the sun sometimes isn't found. But forget the sun, I am around. What can I be?

111. Only the Maker

When you buy me, I am worth nothing. Only the person who makes me know how much it truly costs. Rich kings or the poorest of men give me easily. If I am a broker, deceit and pain can be the results. What will you guess that I am?

112. A Delectable Thing

A most delectable thing, you give me away because you cannot keep me. After you sleep, you may awaken to me as I am soft and moist like a dragonfly wing, but watch out, I can sting. What am I?

113. In a Box

I am contained in a box full of very rare things. No flute. No hair. Would I be? I am very soft in the bed that I won but rock solid. Dim in the dark, I only shine if no longer locked. What would you guess that I am?

114. Moved and Rolled

Moved I can be. Rolled I can be. But you will be able to hold nothing. Blue, red, and other colors I can be even though I don't have a head. I am also eyeless, but I am all over the place. What would you say that I am?

115. Left or Right

Right and left are both ways that I can be used while traveling over bumpy gravel or cobblestone. When used upward, I try for success. When used downwards, I am stressed. What will you say that I am?

116. A Staple Food

You can cook me a lot of different ways, and I come in a lot of different flavors. I'm found in pantries all over the world. Sometimes, it only takes one minute. What am I?

117. Wings Totaling Four

The number of wings I have is four, but I do not fly. My body is able to move around, but I like to stay in the same spot. I chew for a person before they are fed. What am I?

118. First in a Family

My first can be found in family, but not in sweet. The second is in rent, but not in pale. My third is in underwear, but not in town. My fourth is in tiny, but not in scepter. My fifth is in teeth if you look closely. My entire word means a delicious snack for us all. What will you say that I am?

119. Softly Tread

If you walk softly on me, I can take you a gajillion places. I can be very high or very low, and often quite flat in the middle. Kids love me, and adults tolerate me. Figure me out if you can.

120. I Am a Tool

Buy me in the store for a little under or a little over a penny. I am used to inspiring me. Don't overdo me or my effectiveness will no longer be there. Can you tell me what I am?

121. Shifting Around

I only move a small number of inches at a time, but when I move, I go extremely slow. If I move too much, I will be responsible for lots of deaths. Even though I am gigantic, I am not seen by people. Do you know what I am?

122. Women

A few women could care less about being described this way, even though it's a misconception that every woman wants this. It is a crybaby and very loud but transforms when you give it toys. Please tell me what I am.

123. Ancient Stones

I am a bunch of stones put together to protect lots of bones. You can add some riches in there too. I look like a very popular shape. Are you able to say what I am?

124. Glitters

Glitter — yes. Glitter — no. Hot or cold I can be. The eye cannot see my constant changes, but inside me are lots of important things. Some find safety behind me, and others may die under me. Broken I am, old, too, but I bring life forth. What am I if you can guess?

125. Don't Breathe

I jump high and run long even though I don't breathe. I can stretch and swim even though I don't eat. Standing and sleeping are what I do but I do not drink. I may not be able to think, but I can grow and play. Eyeless, I cannot see, but you can see me. Are you able to tell me what I am?

126. Known to Be Deceitful

I once was known as a deceiver despite being held in high esteem. No legs I have, but I can get around and tend to scare lots of people in the process. What am I?

127. More Than Life

Men love me more than life, but they fear me more than death. All men take me to the grave, but the poor have it, rich people don't need me, but if you're content, you're okay with me. Are you able to tell me what I am?

128. Caught in My Trap

You can get caught in my trap because I trap many things of different colors and things. I'm never boring because I change a lot. Can you please tell me what I am?

129. Wealthy

I tend to stand in water and flourish in wealth. I am valued over the land because I am a fencer. I am famous for farmers, but huntsmen despise me. You could possibly experience ruin if I am broken. Can you tell me what I am?

130. First Master

Four legs are how many my first master has. Two legs are how many my second master has. The first master is served in death, and the second master is served in death. I am soft but tough and love to rest on the cheeks of ladies. Are you able to tell me what I am?

131. Weird Creature

I am weird. Words to describe me include straight, metallic, tough, and super long. I puff and squeal and can help a lot of lives move to and from. Can you say what I am?

132. Bleed Without Blood

I do not beat even though I am a heart. No blood, but I can bleed if I am cut. Wingless, I can fly and finless, I can swim. Mouthless, I can sing. Guess what I am.

133. Tender Voice

Slender waist, tender voice, people invite me to play. Everywhere I go, I have to take a bow, or I will have nothing to say. Please tell me what I am if you can.

134. Slippery Fish

I will slip right through your fingers if you are not careful. A spear or a hook cannot catch me, but you'll need to use your hand to capture me. Can you tell me what I am?

135. Love of Mine

I love to see your chalky beauty in whatever formation you are in. If I pay attention, I can see your bright orbs amongst tiny lights. What would you say I am?

136. In My Entirety

In my entirety, I am very safe. If you take my head off, we can meet. If you take my head off, I will be ready. When you put my head back, I become a place for the beasts. Are you able to guess what I am?

137. Two Little Brothers

We are two little brothers. We help some win, and we help some lose. Roll us once, you may like us. Roll us again you may hate us. What can we be?

138. Soft and Cuddly

I am soft and cuddly. I'll put at your heartstrings, but take my last name by itself, and I'll tear you apart. What am I?

139. I Catch Warmth

Who catches heat and traps it? I do. Who brings water and ice to the earth? I do. What can slip through your fingers? I can. What am I?

140. Open Barrel

I look like a piece of honeycomb, but I'm full of soft flesh that is alive. What say you that I am?

141. Keep Things Green

In the summer, I keep many men happy and make children even happier. I bring a life force so strong that the grass loves when I come on. What am I?

142. Red Liquid

Although I am not a safe box, you put a life-saving red fluid inside of me. Please guess what I am.

143. Whoever Makes Me

If I make you, I'm not telling others. If you take me, you'll never know until it's too late. What am I?

144. Empty Inside

I am a useful thing, firm, hard, and white. I am empty inside and can work while being wet or dry. Doctors love me and parents with toddlers hate me. Are you able to guess what I am?

145. English Word

An English word I am. I have 3 sets of double letters in a row. What word am I?

146. Two eyes

Eyes in my front and eyes on my tail, but more eyes on my tail than in the front. Can you guess what I am?

147. Flora

Flora, foliage, and shrubbery are all things that describe me. Fauna, trees, grass are things that do not describe me. Can you tell me what I am?

148. Turn Me Over

Before you sell me, you may turn me over. If you travel far, you may turn me over as well. Can you figure me out?

149. Unique Teeth

I have unique teeth that can get the job done if the hardest force and show of strength does not work. Please, what am I?

150. Fingers Absent

I follow you around all the time even though I once resided in one place. My fingers may be absent, but I have a ring. Please tell me what I am.

Chapter 3: Easy Tricky Riddles

1. Who Am I?

   I am your uncle's sister-in-law and your dad's better half. Who am I?

2. If I state, "Everything I say to you is a lie," is this statement a truthful one or a deceitful lie?

3. Before You Can Get It

   What is one thing that is taken before you can get it?

4. The Last Brick

   To complete one 10-story building made of bricks, how many bricks do you need?

5. Which One

   Phil enjoys tomatoes but hates potatoes. Phil enjoys peas but hates cabbage. Phil enjoys fresh squash but hates onions. Based on Phil's logic of liking the aforementioned, will Phil enjoy oranges or pumpkins?

6. Lucy, the Pet Shop Owner

   Lucy is a pet shop owner who keeps one parrot in a cage with the following signage: "This parrot repeats everything it hears." Someone bought the parrot, but the parrot never said anything back, for two full weeks. The person bought it back, but Lucy said she did not lie about the parrot. How can this be true?

7. Rita Is Trapped

   Rita's enclosed in a room with two ways to leave. A fire-breathing dragon is at the first door. The second way requires you to go through a magnifying glass that will burn you to death if you go through it. Rita is able to get out of the room. How does she do it?

8. Three Different Bags

   Two total marbles are in three separate bags. The first bag has a total of two marbles that are blue. The second bag has a total of two marbles that are green. The third bag has a total of two marbles, but one marble is green, and the other marble is blue. You pick one of the bags randomly and take out a total of one marble that is blue. What is the probability that the remaining marble from the same bag is also blue?

9. A Man on the 11th Floor

   Every day after working on the 11th floor all day, a man takes the elevator to the first floor. However, on the way to work each morning, he takes the elevator up to the 8th floor and then uses the stairs to arrive at the 11th floor, no matter what, unless his colleagues are on the elevator with him or it's raining outside. Explain why he does this.

10. Caught

    After trespassing on the King's hunting property, a person is caught. "You must give me a statement. If the statement is true, you will be killed by lions. If the statement is false, you will be killed by trampling of wild buffalo," the King tells him. After his statement, the man is released. What did the man say to save his life?

11. Traveling the Sea

    How can two sailors standing on opposite sides of the ship, one in the western direction and the other in the eastern direction, still see each other clearly?

12. At an Animal Show

    Recently at an animal show, all of the participants were fish, except two. All of the participants were dogs except two. All of the participants were cats except two. What number of participants are fish, cats, and dogs?

13. No Red Eyes

    No red eyes are allowed in the monastery full of silent monks. The monastery contains no mirrors. If a monk realizes he has eyes that are red, he must leave immediately.

Everyone is okay until someone visits the monastery and states that one monk has eyes that are red. What is the next part of this story?

14. A Fishing Trip

   A fishing trip consists of sons and two dads. Each father and child caught one fish. After arriving at the shore, a total of three fish were in the boat and none of the fish was eaten, thrown into the water, or randomly lost. Explain how this happens.

15. Five Bolts

   Five bolts exist in a row and they are all connected to each other. The first bolt goes in a clockwise direction. In which direction is the fifth bolt turning?

Chapter 4: Hard Tricky Riddles

1. An Island Is Burning

    An island with a forest is burning, and a woman is stranded there. The fire starts on the west side of the island and is quickly burning. There is no way for the woman to put the fire out. She has no hoses or buckets that she can use. She cannot even jump off the island because jagged rocks surround it. If she would jump, it would be certain death. How can she survive?

2. An Intersection

    There is a fork at the road, and you are standing there. In the first direction lies the City of Truth, and the other direction lies the City of Lies. Citizens of the City of Lies always tell lies. Citizens of the City of Truth always tell the truth. A citizen of one of those cities is at the intersection. You have no idea what city the person is from, but you need to ask for help, so you can get to the right place. What is the one question you could ask this person to find out the way to the City of Truth?

3. Friends and Apples

    Ten apples are in a basket that you have. All ten of your
    friends want one. You give every friend one apple because
    you are a very nice person. All your friends thank you for
    your kindness. Now every friend has an apple, but there is
    still an apple in the basket. Explain the way this is possible.
    Think hard, but don't think too long.

4. A Knave, a Knight, and a Spy

    There are three people, (Al, Ben, and Cory), and one of the
    three people is a knave, a spy, and a knight. The knave
    always tells lies, the knight always tells the truth, and truth
    or a lie is what the spy can tell. Al states, "Cody is a knave."
    Ben states, "Alex is a knight." Cory states, "I am the spy."
    Figure out who is the knight, knave, and spy.

5. Two Children

   Two children, one boy and one girl, are talking. "I am a boy," said black-haired kid. "I am a girl," said the white-haired kid. A minimum of one of the kids did not tell the truth. Which child is the boy and which child is the girl?

6. Four Traveling People

   Four people are going various places using various modes of transportation. Rain, Joy, Mr. Johnson, and Candy are their names. The people used train, ship, plane or car. Mr. Johnson hates flying. Candy rents her transportation, and Joy becomes seasick. How did each of them travel?

7. Four More People

   Four more people, Amy, Benton, Cody, and Dennis must cross a stream in a boat. However, the boat carries only 100 pounds, or it will tip over. Amy weighs 90 pounds, Benton weight 80 pounds, Cory weighs 60 pounds and Dennis weighs 40 pounds. They also have 20 pounds of supplies. How do they get across the river?

8. Working at a Fruit Factory

   You see three crates in front of you while on your shift at a factory that produces fruit. The first crate has oranges only. The second crate has apples only. The last crate has a mixture of oranges and apples. However, the machine that does labels is not labeling boxes correctly. The mechanic at your factory is out on vacation so there is no one there to fix the machine. Deliveries still must go on, so you have to figure out what is in what crate. If you are only able to take out one piece of fruit from each crate, how are you able to label all of the boxes correctly?

9. Cannibals

Cannibals in a jungle capture three men. The cannibals will allow the men one chance to get away without being eaten up. The cannibals put the men they captured in a straight line according to their height. The tallest man sees the backs of his two friends. The man in the middle can only see the shortest man's back, and the shortest man cannot see anyone's back. The cannibals give all men the chance to look at five hats of which three are black and two are white. Two hats are white, and three hats are black. The cannibals then cover the men's eyes with blindfolds and put a random hat on the head of every man. The two remaining hats are hidden. The cannibals take the blindfold off and tell the men that if just one can guess what color of hat they are wearing on their head, they can all leave safely. The tallest man in the back says that he cannot guess. The man in the middle says that he cannot also guess. The man in the front says that he knows what hat he is wearing. How so?

10. Forgot Your Socks

You are about to go on a trip, but you forgot your socks. You hurry back up the stairs and rush into your room, but the electricity is off, so you are not able to see any of the colors of your socks. You aren't too worried, because you remember that in your sock baskets, there are a total of 10 pairs of socks that are yellow and ten pairs of socks that are green, and eleven pairs of pink socks, but they are all mixed up. You need to hurry and just grab some socks before you miss your airplane. You paid a lot for your ticket and will not get a refund for a missed flight. How many socks should you put in your bag to assure that at least one pair of the socks is matching?

Chapter 5: Super Easy and Hard Riddles — "What Am I?" Answers

Super Easy Riddles — "What Am I?" Answers

1. Drier, Yet Wetter

Answer: A towel.

2. 3 Miles Away

Answer: The horizon

3. Single Eye

Answer: A needle

4. Black Water

Answer: A lobster

5. Light as a Feather

Answer: Your breath

6. Oceans with No Water

Answer: A Map

7. Two Legs

Answer: A pair of pants

8. Like Bacon and An Egg

Answer: A snake

9. Easy to Get Into
Answer: Trouble

10. Clap and Rumble
Answer: Thunder

11. Neck and No Head
Answer: A bottle

12. Big Bark
Answer: A tree

13. Smooth or Rough Jacket
Answer: A book

14. Up and Down
Answer: A staircase

15. Fly All Day
Answer: A flag

16. Wet Coat
Answer: A coat of paint

17. Unwinnable Bet
Answer: The alphabet

18. Unwearable Dress

Answer: Your address

19. Eyes That Cannot See

Answer: A shoe

20. Serve But Not Eaten

Answer: A tennis ball

21. Limbs, But Cannot Walk

Answer: A tree

22. Come Down But Not Up

Answer: Rain

23. Beat with No Cries

Answer: An egg

24. Travel in One Spot

Answer: A stamp

25. Catch

Answer: A cold

26. Four Eyes

Answer: Mississippi

27. Eighty-eight Keys

Answer: A piano

28. Always Coming

Answer: Tomorrow

29. Careful, Fragile

Answer: A promise

30. Round on Both Sides

Answer: Ohio

31. Lose My Head

Answer: A pillow

32. Hear, But No Body

Answer: Your Voice

33. Rich and Poor People

Answer: Nothing

34. Don't Share

Answer: A secret

35. The More You Take

Answer: A hole

36. Born in the Air

Answer: An echo

37. Millions of Years

Answer: The moon

38. Give It Away

Answer: Your word

39. Stand on One Leg

Answer: A cabbage

40. You Can Throw Me Away

Answer: Corn on the cob

41. Used for Light

Answer: A window

42. Higher Without the Head

Answer: A pillow

43. If I Drink

A fire is the answer.

44. First Letter is Gone

Answer: Empty

45. No Bones or Legs

Answer: An egg

46. Tall When Young

Answer: A candle

47. Throw Me Away

Answer: An anchor

48. When Water Comes
Answer: An umbrella

49. The Maker Doesn't Need Me
Answer: A coffin

50. People Need Me to Eat
Answer: A plate

51. Many Times
Answer: Footsteps

52. End of the Rainbow
Answer: Water

53. Never Ask Questions
Answer: The doorbell

54. No Life
Answer: A battery

55. I Have A Mouth
Answer: A River

56. Lots of Memories
Answer: A photo frame

57. I Go Around and Around

Answer: A street

58. Flying Without Wings

Answer: A cloud

59. No Senses, But I Sense

Answer: A brain

60. Wrong Word

Answer: The word 'wrong'

61. Keys But No Locks

Answer: Keyboard

62. You Take Me

Answer: A pencil

63. Backwards Cheese

Answer: Edam

64. Lots of Letters

Answer: A Post Office

65. A Type of Ship

Answer: A relationship

66. A Mini Tree

Answer: A palm

67. Super Delicate

Answer: Silence

68. One Head, Not Human

Answer: A bed

69. Everyone Needs Me

Answer: Advice

70. What Word

Answer: Shorter

71. A Vehicle

Answer: Racecar

72. What State

Answer: Hawaii

73. Every Night

Answer: Stars

74. Middle of Gravity

The letter 'v' is the answer.

75. Just A Fruit

Answer: Pear

76. No Flaky Hair

Answer: Corn

77. Pilgrim Music

Answer: Plymouth Rock

78. Dangerous

Answer: Words

79. A Man's Weakness

Answer: Sleep

80. I Belong to You

Answer: Your Name

81. I Can Be Long or Short

Answer: A fingernail

82. I Have Just One

Answer: A cat

83. Men and Women

Answer: Music

84. Container with No Hinges

Answer: An egg

85. One Color

Answer: A shadow

86. Reach for the Sky

Answer: A tree

87. I Have Three Letters

Answer: Eye

88. Sometimes White, Sometimes Black

Answer: A hearse

89. Red or Green

Answer: Peppers

90. Many Legs

Answer: A broom

91. An Insect

Answer: Beetle

92. Many Feathers

Answer: An arrow

93. A Potato's Tool

Answer: A TV remote control

94. No Lungs

Answer: Fire

95. First in the Ocean

Answer: An owl

96. Very Skinny

Answer: A tornado

97. Invisible, Yet There

Answer: A soul

98. Slim and Tall

Answer: A cigarette

99. To Measure or Not to Measure

Answer: Time

100. White and Grind

Answer: Teeth

101. Walk on Four Legs

Answer: Man

102. Cannot Control Me

Answer: A baby

103. Can't Catch Me

Answer: Wind

104. One Blind Eye

Answer: A hurricane

105. Different Colors

Answer: Charcoal

106. Pointed Teeth
Answer: A stapler

107. No eyes
Answer: A skull

108. Weight in My Belly
Answer: A ship

109. Cannot Be Seen
Answer: Darkness

110. Light and Hidden
Answer: An iceberg

111. Between Your Head and Toes
Answer: A bar of soap

112. Different Sizes and Shapes
Answer: A jigsaw puzzle piece

113. Sleep in The Day
Answer: A bat

114. Travel Low and High
Answer: Musical Notes

115. None Seeps

Answer: Your skin

116. Thirty Men

Answer: A chess match

117. Often Held

Answer: A person's tongue

118. Up and Down

Answer: A see-saw

119. Tear Me Off

Answer: Matches

120. No Fingers

Answer: A wheelbarrow

121. Crack A Smile

Answer: A mirror

122. Always Old

Answer: The Moon

123. Loud Noise

Answer: Popcorn

124. You Hear

Answer: An echo

125. What Letter

Answer: The letter 'R'

126. Ruler of Shovels

Answer: The King from the Spades suite

127. Four Fingers

Answer: A glove

128. The Pope Does Not Use It

Answer: A last name

129. Invisible Roots

Answer: A mountain

130. Nothing on the Outside

Answer: A bubble

131. Beauty in the Sky

Answer: A rainbow

132. No Drinks from This Fountain

Answer: Oil

133. A Precious Stone

Answer: Ice

134. I Beam

Answer: A smile

135. I Devour
Answer: Time

136. I Am Small
Answer: A hummingbird

137. I Am Big
Answer: An elephant

138. I March Before Armies
Answer: A flag

139. Start of All Ideas
Answer: Paper

140. My Children
Answer: Sun

141. I Can Fall
Answer: Water

142. Stop and Look
Answer: Horizon
143. You Have Me
Answer: Memories

144. In You

Answer: Water

145. Cracked

Answer: A joke

146. I Am Red

Answer: A heart

147. Sweet Rest

Answer: A pillow

148. Soup or Burger

Answer: A tomato

149. Children Love Me

Answer: A kite

150. The Ocean Is My Hand

Answer: A fish

151. Don't Drop Me

Answer: A cellphone

152. I Wiggle

Answer: A worm

153. A Special Room

Answer: A mushroom

154. Wave Me

Answer: A fan

155. Three Eyes

Answer: A traffic light

156. Forward and Backward

Answer: A rocking chair

157. Long Tail

Answer: A mouse

158. Carry Me

Answer: An umbrella

159. No Voice

Answer: A book

160. Different Colors

Answer: Flowers

161. Bigger When Full

Answer: A balloon

162. Brick Body

Answer: A house

163. Keep Me Away

Answer: Scissors

164. Easily Overlooked

Answer: A nose

165. The Harder You Run

Answer: Your breath

166. Twirl My Body

Answer: A screw

167. Seed

Answer: A pea

168. Going Up

Answer: Your age

169. Green Jacket

Answer: Watermelon

170. Black as Night

Answer: A bowling ball

171. Good at Hiding

Answer: Makeup

172. Pure, But Forgotten

Answer: Air

173. I Ran

Answer: An Hourglass

174. A Mother

Answer: Earth

175. Never Stolen

Answer: Knowledge

176. Enjoyed by Some

Answer: Marriage

177. Soft and Hairy

Answer: Carpet

178. A Ring

Answer: Telephone

179. Take Off My Clothes

Answer: A clothes hanger

180. Metal or Bone

Answer: A comb

181. Run Around

Answer: A shoe

182. The Protector

Answer: Sunglasses

183. An Absolute Necessity

Answer: Coffee

184. Not Born

Answer: A clone

185. In the Rainforest

Answer: A sloth

186. Buttons or a Zipper

Answer: A coat

187. Jump and Climb

Answer: A spider

188. Go Up

Answer: A ball

189. Keep You Entertained

Answer: A television

190. Curly and Bald

Answer: Hair

191. In the Woods

Answer: A splinter

192. Wake You

Answer: A rooster

193. Lick, Lick

Answer: Ice cream

194. A Fruit

Answer: A date

195. Two Meanings

Answer: A tie

196. A Food

Answer: Wheat

197. I Am Scary

Answer: Smoke

198. A Small Piece of Paper

Answer: A ticket

199. Can Be Embarrassing

Answer: Scale

200. People Walk in Me

Answer: An elevator

Hard "What Am I?" Riddle Answers

1. Beginning of the End

Answer: The letter 'e' is the first letter of 'end' and the last letter of 'place.' 'E' also is the first letter of 'eternity' and the last letter of the words 'space' and 'time.'

2. First

Answer: A badger

3. Creature of Power

Answer: Tree

4. Two Sisters

Answer: Salt and pepper

5. Four-Letter Word

Answer: Noon

6. The Traveling Letter

Answer: T

7. Covered in White

Answer: Frost

8. White and Dirty

Answer: A chalkboard

9. Hard Tongue

Answer: A bell

10. Letters Equal to Six

Answer: Member

11. Three Lives

Answer: Water

12. Sky and the Ground

Answer: Leaf

13. Fall and Break

Answer: Day and Night

14. Water of Life

Answer: Blood

15. Forward

Answer: Ton

16. Feel Me, But Can't See

Answer: Your fears

17. Bat with Me

Answer: Eyelashes

18. Red Tears

Answer: A cherry

19. Use Me Everyday

Answer: Your feet

20. Creative Memories

Answer: Music

21. Served at a Table

Answer: Ping pong balls

22. Out the Earth

Answer: An onion

23. Dog's Name

Answer: K9

24. Straight Through Me

Answer: The blink of an eye

25. I Am Not Magic

Answer: Mirror

26. Share, But Selfish

Answer: Knowledge

27. I Am Two

Answer: The letter 'r'

28. Thunder Before Lightning

Answer: A volcano

29. Five and Six

Answer: A clock

30. Give Me Away

Answer: Money

31. Starts with Gas

Answer: An automobile

32. Shave Beards

Answer: A barber

33. Hides at Night

Answer: A fly

34. There Is a Word

Answer: Heroine

35. In the Past

Answer: History

36. See Me in Water

Answer: A reflection

37. My Brother

Answer: Thunder and lightning

38. I Travel Alone

Answer: A shadow

39. Summertime Favorite

Answer: A marshmallow

40. Sweet or Sour

Answer: Orange

41. Compliments People

Answer: Hand

42. A Simple Circle

Answer: Zero

43. Two in a Whole

Answer: Half

44. Digging a Tiny Cave

Answer: A dentist

45. Simple or Complex

Answer: A pattern

46. Some People

Answer: Calories

47. It May Sound

Answer: A busboy

48. A Shimmering Field

Answer: Ocean

49. Write on Me

Answer: A floppy disk

50. Folding

Answer: A Paper Cut

51. Two Occupants

Answer: A peanut

52. Walking and Running

Answer: A treadmill

53. Not My Name

Answer: Tombstone

54. In Window

Answer: Dove

55. You Can't Hide

Answer: Death

56. I Am Brown

Answer: A saddle

57. The Path

Answer: A valley

58. Once A God
Answer: A cat

59. Soft Like Silk
Answer: Cotton

60. Two-faced
Answer: A coin

61. Very Tempting
Answer: An apple

62. When Young
Answer: Wine

63. My Title
Answer: A knight

64. Head Bob
Answer: A daisy

65. Perfect with a Head
Answer: A wig

66. Add the Letter S
Answer: Dice

67. More Shoes

Answer: The ground

68. Your Mechanic's Name

Answer: Will

69. Beneath Your Roof

Answer: Wood

70. Cut Through Evil

Answer: Justice

71. I Have Two

Answer: Sharing

72. Something Sweet

Answer: Kitchen

73. Busy Street

Answer: Parking meter

74. I Heard of a Wonder

Answer: A bookworm

75. Moving Slow

Answer: Your hair

76. Take a Spin

Answer: A Fan

77. Bury Me

Answer: A plant

78. I Can Help You See

Answer: Sand

79. Born of Water

Answer: A mosquito

80. Everyone Faces Me

Answer: A birthday

81. Silver-tongued

Answer: Mercury (This element of the periodic table looks wet, shiny, and silver. Also, the god Mercy has two wings but only uses them to run.)

82. Twelve Is Left

Answer: Dozens

83. White Father, Black Child

Answer: Smoke

84. Alive Without A Breath

Answer: Fish

85. Visible to You

Answer: Time

86. Speak the Truth

Answer: A book

87. Airy Creatures

Answer: Vowels

88. Peep, Peep

Answer: A star

89. A Utensil

Answer: A knife

90. A Hundred Years

Answer: A tree

91. Helping Engines

Answer: A belt

92. They Belong to Me

Answer: Thoughts

93. I Am Round

Answer: Football

94. Beautiful and Cold

Answer: A vampire

95. Lovely and Round

Answer: A pear

96. End of My Yard

Answer: Flax

97. Makes No Sense

Answer: Dreams

98. First a Blessing

Answer: A rainbow

99. Used for Light

Answer: A window

100. Backbite

Answer: A flea

101. I Can Wave

Answer: An electric fan

102. Forest Without Trees

Answer: The zoo

103. Heavy Feet

Answer: The gallows

104. Sleeping During the Day

Answer: Sunrise

105. Lacking Reason

Answer: A Riddle

106. I Drink

Answer: A pen

107. A Tradition

Answer: Alchemy

108. Small and Light

Answer: A lighter

109. Four Legs

Answer: A desk

110. Every Dawn

Answer: The letter 'D'

111. Only the Maker

Answer: A promise

112. A Delectable Thing

Answer: A kiss

113. In a Box

Answer: Jewel

114. Moved and Rolled

Answer: A ball

115. Left or Right
Answer: A thumb

116. A Staple Food
Answer: Rice

117. Four Wings
Answer: A windmill

118. First in Family
Answer: Fruit

119. Softly Tread
Answer: Stairs

120. I Am A Tool
Answer: A pen

121. Shifting Around
Answer: A tectonic plate

122. Women
Answer: A baby

123. Ancient
Answer: Pyramids

124. Glitters

Answer: Rock

125. Don't Breathe

Answer: Leg

126. Known to Be Deceitful

Answer: Snake

127. More Than Life

Answer: Nothing

128. Caught in My Trap

Answer: A mirror

129. In Wealth

Answer: A bank

130. First Master

Answer: Fur

131. Weird Creature

Answer: A train

132. Bleed Without Blood

Answer: Wood

133. Tender Voice

Answer: Violin

134. A Slippery Fish

Answer: Soap

135. My Love
Answer: Moon

136. In My Entirety
Answer: A stable

137. Two Little Brothers
Answer: Dice

138. Soft and Cuddly
Answer: A teddy bear

139. I Catch Warmth
Answer: Clouds

140. Open Barrel
Answer: A thimble

141. Keep Things Green
Answer: A sprinkler

142. Red Liquid
Answer: Blood bank

143. Whoever Makes Me
Answer: Poison

144. Empty Inside

Answer: A pen

145. English Word

Answer: Bookkeeper

146. Two Eyes

Answer: A peacock

147. Flora

Answer: Bush

148. Turn Me Over

Answer: Odometer

149. Unique Teeth

Answer: A key

150. No Fingers

Answer: Telephone

Chapter 6: Tricky Riddles' Answers

Easy Tricky Riddles' Answers

1. Who Am I?

   Answer: Your mother

2. If

   Answer: A lie

3. Before You Can Get It

   Answer: A picture

4. How Many Bricks

   Answer: Just one. The 'last' brick completes the building.

5. Which One

   Answer: Pumpkins. Terry only likes foods that grow on vines.

6. Lucy, The Pet Shop Owner

   Answer: Lucy didn't lie because the parrot was deaf.

7. Rita Is Trapped

   Answer: Rita escapes by waiting until night time and going through the second door.

8. Three Different Bags

   Answer: There is a 2/3 chance, not 1/2 chances. You know that you did not big from Bag B with the two green marbles, so you have three possibilities. You chose Bag A, first blue marble. The other marble will be blue. You chose Bag A, second blue marble. The other marble will be blue. You chose Bag C, the blue marble. So, the other marble will be green. So, 2 out of 3 possibilities are blue. The answer is not 1/2 because you are selecting marbles, not bags.

9. A Man on the 11th Floor

   Answer: The man is too short to reach the '20' button. However, when other people are on the elevator with him, he can ask them to push the button for the 2oth floor. On a rainy day, he has an umbrella, so he can push the button using that.

10. Caught

    Answer: "I will be killed by trampling of wild buffalo." The King is unable to say that is the correct answer because if that answer is true, the man will need to be killed by lions. But if the man is killed by the lions, then his answer is not the truth, and he will need to be stomped on by the buffalo. So, the king just let the man go.

11. Traveling the Sea

    Answer: The sailors had their backs turned to either end of the ship.

12. At an Animal Show

Answer: There are only three total animals at the show — one dog, one cat, and one fish. If all the animals were there except for two, then that would satisfy the requirements of the riddle.

13. No Red Eyes

Answer: If there is only one monk with a red eye, he will see the monk and know he is the one with the eye that is red and will leave. If there are two, one will see the red eye and stay. If the second monk sees the man staying, the next morning, he will know that he has the red eye. So on and so forth.

14. A Fishing Trip

Answer: The trip consists of a total of three people: the son, father, and his grandfather.

15. Five Bolts

Answer: It is rotating clockwise.

Hard Tricky Riddles' Answers

1. A Burning Island

    Answer: The woman will quickly get a stick and set fire to
    the eastern side of the island. The wind will cause the fires
    to cancel each other out and she can stay in the burnt part
    until the fire is finished. However, even though she is
    capable of surviving the fire, she will die by starving
    because the fire will leave absolutely no food that she can
    eat. She also would not be able to drink the sea water.
    Worst-case scenario, she could drink her urine, but at some
    point, she would still be left with no food or a way to
    survive unless someone rescues her.

2. An Intersection

    Answer: You will ask, "What direction do you live?" A
    Citizen of the City of Truth will point to the City of Truth.
    A Citizen of the City of Lies will point to the City of Truth.
    From their answer, you will know which way to go in order
    to arrive at your destination.

3. Friends and Apples

    Answer: You gave an apple to the first nine friends, and
    then gave the apple in the basket to the last friend, thus the
    last apple in the basket is the apple of the tenth friend.

4. A Knave, A Knight, and a Spy

    Answer: Al is a knight. Ben is a spy, and Cory is a knave.
    Ben is not the knight since if he was, Al would be the
    knight, too. Cory is not the knight since his statement

186

would automatically be a lie. So, Al equals the knight. Cory equals the knave, and Ben equals the spy.

5. A Girl and a Boy

    Answer: They both told a lie. The child with the black hair is the girl, and the child with the white hair is the boy. If only one of them lied, they would both be girls, or both would be boys.

6. Four Traveling People

    Answer: There are three different possibilities.
    1. Candy — car; Mr. Johnson — train; Joy — plane; Rain — ship
    2. Candy — car; Mr. Johnson — ship; Joy — plane; Rain — train
    3. Candy — car; Mr. Johnson — ship; Joy — train; Rain — plane

7. Four More People

    Answer: Cody and Dennis row across; Dennis returns. Amy rows over and Cody returns. Cody and Dennis row across again, Dennis returns. Benton rows across with the supplies and Cody returns. Cody and Dennis row across again for the last time.

8. Working at a Fruit Factory

    Answer: You should start by taking a piece of fruit from the crate that states 'oranges and apples.' If an apple is pulled out, then you know that it is the apples' crate since all the labels are not correct. So, the crate that states 'apples' must really be 'oranges' and the one marked 'oranges' must really be the 'oranges and apples' crate. If you pull out an orange, you will follow the same logic, just use the opposite of what was aforementioned.

9. Cannibals

Answer: The man at the front is wearing a black hat because he knows that the tallest man could not see hats that were all white. The middle man did not see a white hat, because if he would have seen a white hat, the middle man would have known that his hat was black from hearing what the first man said.

10. Forgot Your Socks

Answer: The correct answer is four. Although there are lots of socks in the drawer, there are only three colors, so if you take four socks, then you are assured to have one pair that matches.

Conclusion

Thanks for making it through to the end of *The King of Riddles*. Let's hope it was informative and able to provide you with all of the tools you need to achieve your goals whatever they may be. You may start to see amazing results from doing these riddles such as improving your thought process and how you feel when solving difficult problems. Don't fret! Just enjoy it.

The next step is to keep practicing in order to improve and enjoy the benefits of doing riddles. You can research for more riddles or even try your hand at creating riddles for all your family and friends to solve. You can even go back and review the riddles you found that were the trickiest in this book. Or you can challenge others with the riddles that were the hardest for you to see how they react. Whatever you do, just keep practicing. As the cliché says, "Practice makes perfect," and in this case, it is definitely true.

Finally, if you found this book useful in any way, a review on Amazon is always appreciated!

Catch us on Facebook www.facebook.com/bluesourceandfriends

Don't forget to claim your FREE book
https://tinyurl.com/karenbrainteasers

Karen J. Bun

Printed in Great Britain
by Amazon